PIC C

An introduction to programming the Microchip PIC in CCS C

by Nigel Gardner & Mark Siegesmund

Typeset and printed in the UK by: Character Press Limited.
Tel: 01462 896500. First printed in 1998.

Circuit diagrams produced with Labcentre Isis Illustrator. Flowcharts produced with Corel Flow.

Preface

Thanks go to Rodger Richey of Microchip Technology Inc. for the use of his notes on C for the PICmicro, Mark at CCS and Val Bellamy for proof reading this book.

This book is dedicated to my wife June and daughter Emma.

Contents

Introduction

Why use C?

The C language was developed at the Bell Labs in the late 60's by Dennis Ritchie and Brian Kernighan. One of the first platforms for implementation was the PDP-11 running under a UNIX environment. Since its introduction, it has evolved and been standardised throughout the computing industry as an established development language. The PC has become a cost effective development platform using C++ or other favoured versions of the ANSII standard.

C is a portable language intended to have minimal modification when transferring programs from one computer to another. This is fine when working with PC's and mainframes, but Microcontrollers and Microprocessors are a different breed. The main program flow will basically remain unchanged, but the various setup and port / peripheral control will be micro specific. An example of this is that the port direction registers on a PIC are set 1=Input 0=Output, whereas the H8 is 0=Input and 1=Output.

The use of C in Microcontroller applications has been brought about by manufacturers providing larger program and ram memory areas in addition to faster operating speeds.

An example quoted to me - as a non believer - was: to create a stopclock function would take 2/3 days in C or 2 weeks in assembler. 'Ah' I hear you say as you rush to buy a C compiler - why do we bother to write in assembler? It comes down to code efficiency - a program written in assembler is typically 80% the size of a C version. Fine on the larger program memory sized devices but not so efficient on smaller devices. You pay the money and take your PIC!!

PC Based versus PIC Based Program Development

Engineers starting development on PC based products have the luxuary of basic hardware pre-wired i.e. keyboard, processor, memory, I/O, printer and visual display (screen). The product development then comes down to writing the software and debugging the errrrrrus.

Those embarking on a PIC based design have to create all the interface to the outside world in the form of input and output hardware. A PC programmer could write the message `"Hello World"` and after compiling, have the message displayed on the screen. The PIC programmer would have to build an RS232 interface, set up the comm port within the PIC and attach the development board to a comm port on a PC to enable the message to be viewed.

'Why bother' I hear you say (and so did I) - it comes down to portability of the end product. If we could get the whole of a PC in a 40 pin DIL package (including monitor and keyboard) we would use it, but as today's miniaturisation does not reach these limits, we will continue to use microcontrollers like the PIC for low cost and portable applications.

The development tools for PIC based designs offer the developer basically the same facilities as the PC based development with the exception of the graphics libraries.

PRODUCT DEVELOPMENT

Product development is a combination of luck and experience. Some of the simplest tasks can take a long time to develop and perfect in proportion to the overall product - so be warned where tight timescales are involved.

To design a product one needs: time - peace and quiet - a logical mind and most important of all a full understanding of the requirements.

I find the easiest way to begin any development is to start with a clean sheet of paper together with the specification or idea.

Start by drawing out a number of possible solutions and examine each to try to find the simplest and most reliable option. Don't discard the other ideas at this stage as there are possibly some good thoughts there.

Draw out a flow chart, block diagram, I/O connection plan or any suitable drawing to get started.

Build up a prototype board or hardware mimic board with all the I/O configured. Don't forget i/o pins can be swapped to make board layout easier at a later date - usually with minimal modification to the software.

Then start writing the code - in testable blocks - and gradually build up your program. This saves trying to debug 2000 lines of code in one go!

If this is your first project - THEN KEEP IT SIMPLE - try out just switching a LED or two on and off from push buttons to get familiar with the instructions, assembly technique and debugging before attempting a mammoth project.

Build up the program in simple stages - testing as you go. Rework your flowchart to keep it up to date.

THE IDEA

An idea is born - maybe by yourself in true EUREKA style or by someone else having a need for a product - the basic concept is the same.

Before the design process starts, the basic terminology needs to be understood - like learning a new language. So in the case of Microcontroller designs based on the PIC, the PIC language (instruction set, terms and development kit) needs to be thoroughly understood before the design can commence.

Now let's get started with the general terms, some facts about the PIC and the difference between Microprocessor and Microcontroller based systems.

Terminology

Let's start with some basic terminology used.

Microcontroller A lump of plastic, metal and purified sand which, without any software, does nothing When software controls a microcontroller, it has almost unlimited applications.

I/O A connection pin to the outside world which can be configured as input or output. I/O is needed in most cases to allow the microcontroller to communicate, control or read information.

Software The information that the Microcontroller needs to operate or run. This needs to be free of bugs and errors for a successful application or product. Software can be written in a variety of languages such as C, Pascal or Assembler (one level up from writing your software in binary).

Hardware The Microcontroller, memory, interface components, power supplies, signal conditioning circuits and all the components - connected to it to make it work and interface to the outside world. Another way of looking at (especially when it does not work) is that you can kick hardware.

Simulator The MPLAB development environment has its own inbuilt simulator which allows access to some of the internal operation of the microcontroller. This is a good way of testing your designs if you know when events occur. If an event occurs 'somewhere about there', you might find the simulator restrictive. Full trace, step and debug facilities are, however, available. Another product for 16C5x development is the SIM ICE - a hardware simulator offering some of the ICE features but at a fraction of the cost.

In Circuit Emulator (ICEPIC or PIC MASTER) - a very useful piece of equipment connected between your PC and the socket where the Microcontroller will reside. It enables the software to be run on the PC but looks like a Microcontroller at the circuit board end. The ICE allows you to step through a program, watch what happens within the micro and how it communicates with the outside world.

Programmer A unit to enable the program to be loaded into the microcontroller's memory which allows it to run without the aid of an ICE. They come in all shapes and sizes and costs vary. Both the PICSTART PLUS and PROMATE II from Microchip connect to the serial port.

Source File A program written in a language the assembler and you understand. The source file has to be processed before the Microcontroller will understand it.

Assembler / Compiler A software package which converts the Source file into an Object file. Error checking is built in, a heavily used feature in debugging a program as errors are flagged up during the assembly process. MPASM is the latest assembler from Microchip handling all the PIC family.

Object File This is a file produced by the Assembler / Compiler and is in a form which the programmer, simulator or ICE understands to enable it to perform its function. File extension is .OBJ or .HEX depending on the assembler directive.

List File This is a file created by the Assembler /Compiler and contains all the instructions from the Source file together with their hexadecimal values alongside and comments you have written. This is the most useful file to examine when trying to debug the program as you have a greater chance of following what is happening within the software than the Source file listing. The file extension is .LST

Other Files The error file (.ERR) contains a list of errors but does not give any indication as to their origin. The .COD file is used by the emulator.

Bugs Errors created free of charge by you. These range from simpel typin errus to incorrect use of the software language syntax errors. Most of these bugs will be found by the compiler and shown up in a .LST file, others will have to be sought and corrected by trial and error.

Microprocessor

A microprocessor or digital computer is made up of three basic sections: CPU, I/O and Memory - with the addition of some support circuitry.

Each section can vary in complexity from the basic to all bells and whistles.

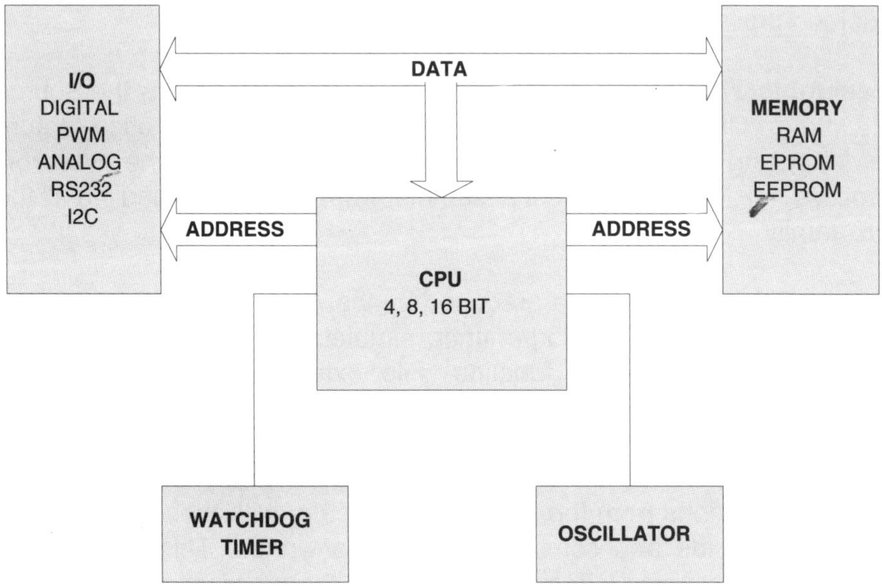

TYPICAL MICROPROCESSOR SYSTEM

Taking each one in turn:-

Input/output (I/O) can comprise digital, analogue and special functions and is the section which communicates with the outside world.

The central processor unit (CPU) is the heart of the system and can work in 4, 8 or 16 bit data formats to perform the calculations and data manipulation.

The memory can be RAM, ROM, EPROM, EEPROM or any combination of these and is used to store the program and data.

An oscillator is required to drive the microprocessor. Its function is to clock data and instructions into the CPU, compute the results and then output the information. The oscillator can be made from discrete components or be a ready made module.

Other circuitry found associated with the microprocessor are the watch dog timer - to help prevent system latchup, buffering for address and data busses to allow a number of chips to be connected together without deteriorating the logic levels and decode logic for address and I/O to select one of a number of circuits connected on the same bus.

It is normal to refer to a Microprocessor as a product which is mainly the CPU area of the system. The I/O and memory would be formed from separate chips and require a Data Bus, Address Bus and Address Decoding to enable correct operation.

Microcontrollers

The PIC, on the other hand, is a Microcontroller and has all the CPU, memory, oscillator, watchdog and I/O incorporated within the same chip. This saves space, design time and external peripheral timing and compatibility problems, but in some circumstances can limit the design to a set memory size and I/O capabilities.

The PIC family of microcontrollers offers a wide range of I/O, memory and special functions to meet most requirements of the development engineer.

You will find many general books on library shelves exploring the design of microcontrollers, microprocessors and computers, so the subject will not be expanded or duplicated here other than to explain the basic differences.

Why use the PIC?

Code Efficiency The PIC is an 8 bit Microcontroller based on the Harvard architecture - which means there are separate internal busses for memory and data. The throughput rate is therefore increased due to simultaneous access to both data and program memory. Conventional microcontrollers tend to have one internal bus handling both data and program. This slows operation down by at least a factor of 2 when compared to the PIC.

Safety All the instructions fit into a 12 or 14 bit program memory word. There is no likelihood of the software jumping into the DATA section of a program and trying to execute DATA as instructions. This can occur in a non Harvard architecture microcontroller using 8-bit busses.

Instruction Set There are 33 instructions you have to learn in order to write software for the 16C5x family and 35 for the 16Cxx devices. All the instructions used by the PIC are based on registers and are 12 bits in length for the 16C5x family and 14 bits wide for the l6Cxx family. Each instruction, with the exception of CALL, GOTO or bit testing instructions (BTFSS, INCFSZ), executes in one cycle.

Speed The PIC has an internal divide by 4 connected between the oscillator and the internal clock bus. This makes instruction time easy to calculate, especially if you use a 4 MHz crystal. Each instruction cycle then works out at 1 uS. The PIC is a very fast micro to work with e.g. a 20MHz crystal steps through a program at 5 million instructions per second! - almost twice the speed of a 386SX 33!

Static Operation The PIC is a fully static microprocessor; in other words, if you stop the clock, all the register contents are maintained. In practice you would not actually do this, you would place the PIC into a Sleep mode - this stops the clock and sets up various flags within the PIC to allow you to know what state it was in before the Sleep. In Sleep, the PIC takes only its standby current which can be less the 1 uA.

Drive Capability The PIC has a high output drive capability and can directly drive LEDs and triacs etc. Any I/O pin can sink 25mA, or 100mA for the whole device.

Options A range of speed, temperature, package, I/O lines, timer functions, serial comms, A/D and memory sizes is available from the PIC family to suit virtually all your requirements.

Versatility The PIC is a versatile micro and in volume is a low cost solution to replace even a few logic gates; especially where space is at a premium

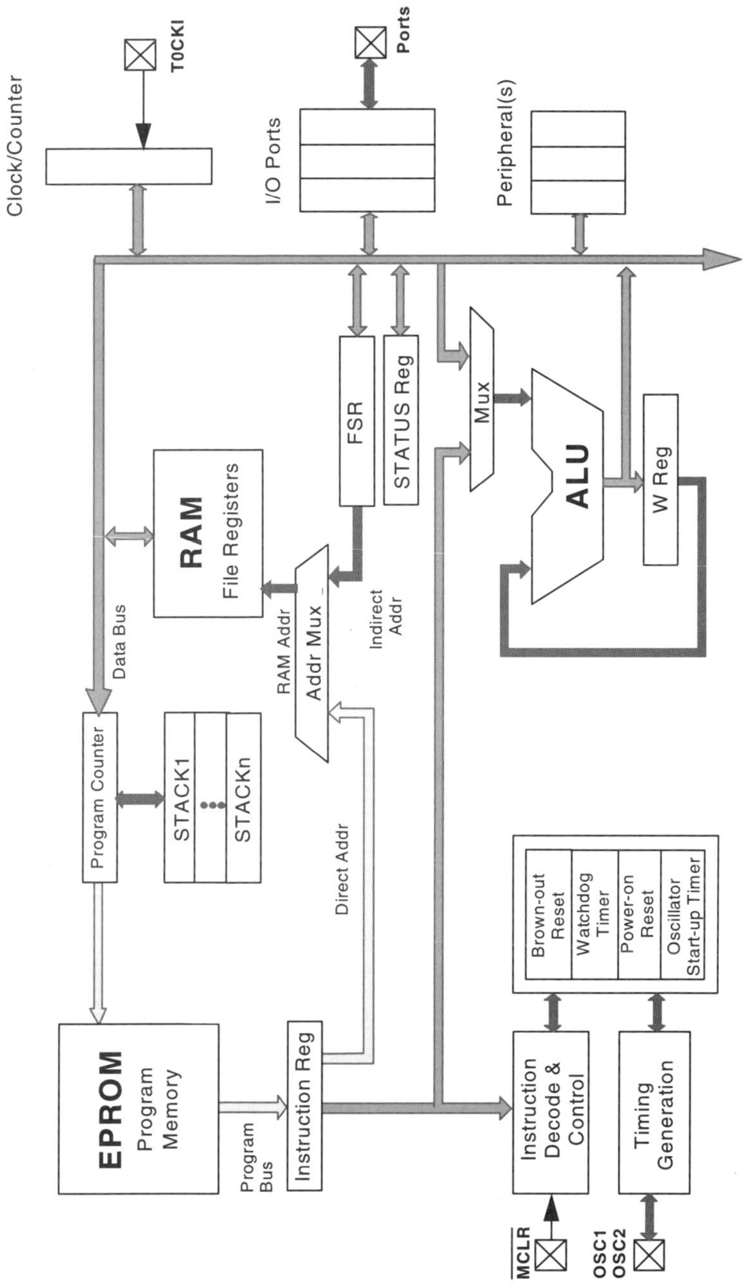

BASIC PIC BLOCK DIAGRAM

Security The PIC has a code protection facility which is one of the best in the industry. Once the protection bit has been programmed, the contents of the program memory cannot be read out in a way that the program code can be reconstructed.

Development The PIC is available in windowed form for development and OTP (one time programmable) for production. The tools for development are readily available and are very affordable even for the home enthusiast

Trying and Testing Code

Getting to grips with C can be a daunting task and the initial outlay for a C compiler, In Circuit Emulator and necessary hardware for the PIC can be prohibitive at the evaluation stage of a project. The C compiler supplied on this disk was obtained from the Internet and is included as a test bed for code learning. Basic code examples and functions can be tried, tested and viewed before delving into PIC specific C compilers which handle I/O etc.

C Coding Standards

Program writing is like building a house - if the foundations are firm, the rest of the code will stack up. If the foundations are weak, the code will fall over at some point or other. The following recommendations were taken from a C++ Standards document and have been adapted for the PIC.

Names - make them fit their function
Names are the heart of programming so make a name appropriate to its function and what it's used for in the program.
Use mixed case names to improve the readability

```
ErrorCheck is easier than ERRORCHECK
```

Prefix names with a lowercase letter of their type, again to improve readability:-

g Global	`gLog;`
r Reference	`rStatus();`
s Static	`sValueIn;`

Braces {}

Braces or curly brackets can be used in the traditional UNIX way

```
if (condition) {
........
}
```

or the preferred method which is easier to read

```
if (condition)
{
........
}
```

Tabs and Indentation

Use spaces in place of tabs as the normal tab setting of 8 soon uses up the page width. Indent text only as needed to make the software readable. Also, tabs set in one editor may not be the same settings in another - make the code portable.

Line Length

Keep line lengths to 78 characters for compatibility between monitors and printers.

Else If Formatting

Include an extra Else statement to catch any conditions not covered by the preceding if's

```
if (condition)
{
}
else if (condition)
{
}
else
{
.......   /* catches anything else not covered above
}
```

Condition Format

Where the compiller allows it, always put the constant on the left hand side of an equality / inequality comparison. If one = is omitted, the compiler will find the error for you. The value is also placed in a prominent place.

```
if (6== ErrorNum) ...
```

Initialise All Variables

Set all variables to a known values to prevent 'floating or random conditions' `int a=6, b=0;`

Comments

Comments create the other half of the story you are writing. You know how your program operates today but in two weeks or two years will you remember, or could someone else follow your program as it stands today?

Use comments to mark areas where further work needs to be done, errors to be debugged or future enhancements to the product.

Basics

All computer programs have a start. The start point in Microcontrollers is the reset vector. The 14 bit core (PIC16Cxx family) reset at 00h, the 12 bit core (PIC16C5x and 12C50x) reset at the highest point in memory - 1FFh, 3FFh, 7FFh.

The finish point would be where the program stops if run only once e.g. a routine to set up a baud rate for communications. Other programs will loop back towards the start point such as traffic light control. One of the most widely used first programming examples in high level languages like Basic or C is printing 'Hello World' on the computer screen.

Using C and a PC is straightforward as the screen, keyboard and processor are all interconnected. The basic hooks need to be placed in the program to link the program to the peripherals. When developing a program for the PIC or any microprocessor / microcontroller system, you need not only the software hooks but also the physical hardware to connect the micro to the outside world. Such a system is shown below.

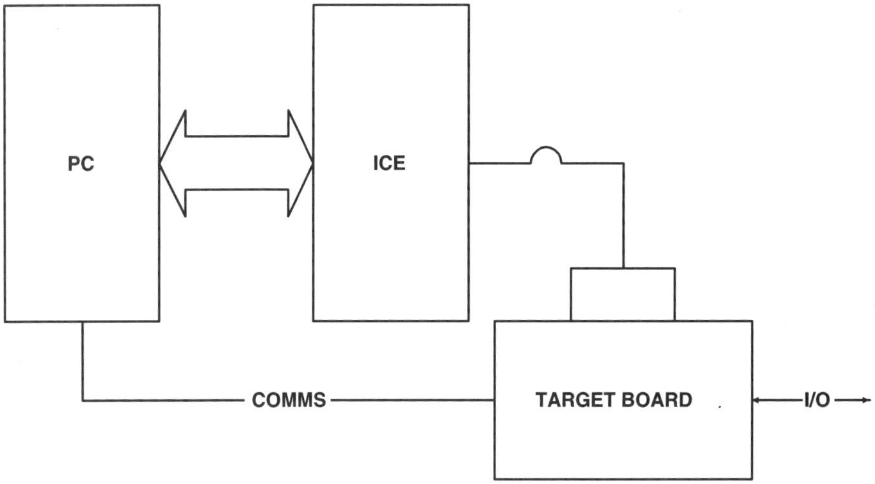

Using such a layout enables basic I/O and comms to be evaluated, tested and debugged. The use of the ICE, though not essential, speeds up the development process many fold and so reduces the overall development costs and engineer's headaches. The initial investment may appear excessive when facing the start of a project, but time saved in developing and debugging is soon outstripped.

The hardware needed to evaluate a design can be a custom made PCB, protoboard or an off the shelf development board such as our PIC Millennium Board (someone had to do one!) The Millennium board contains all the basic hardware to enable commencement of most designs while keeping the initial outlay to a minimum.

Assemble the following hardware in whichever format you prefer. You WILL need a PIC programmer such as the PICSTART Plus as a minimal outlay in addition to the C compiler.

A simple program I use when teaching engineers about the PIC is the 'Press button - turn on LED'. Start with a simple code example - not 2000 lines of code!
In Assembler this would be :-

```
main   btfss porta,switch    ; test for switch closure
       goto  main            ; loop until pressed
```

```
      bsf   portb,led        ; turn on led
lp1   btfsc porta,switch; test for switch open
      goto  lp1              ; loop until released
      bcf   portb,led        ; turn off led
      goto  main           ; loop back to start
```

In C this converts to

```
main()
{
   set_tris_b(0x00);               // set port b as outputs

     while(true)
     {
      if (input(PIN_A0))           // test for switch closure
      output_high(PIN_B0);         // if closed turn on led
      else
        output_low(PIN_B0);        // if open turn off led
     }
}
```

When assembled, the code looks like this:-

```
      main()
      {
      set_tris_b(0x00);
                        0007  MOVLW  00
                        0008  TRIS   6
      while(true)
        {
        if (input(PIN_A0))
                        0009  BTFSS  05,0
                        000A  GOTO   00D
        output_high(PIN_B0);
                        000B  BSF    06,0
        else
                        000C  GOTO   00E
        output_low(PIN_B0);
                        000D  BCF    06,0
        }
                        000E  GOTO   009
      }
```

As you can see, the compiled version takes more words in memory - 14 in C as opposed to 9 in Assembler. This is not a fair example on code but as programs get larger, the more efficient C becomes in code usage.

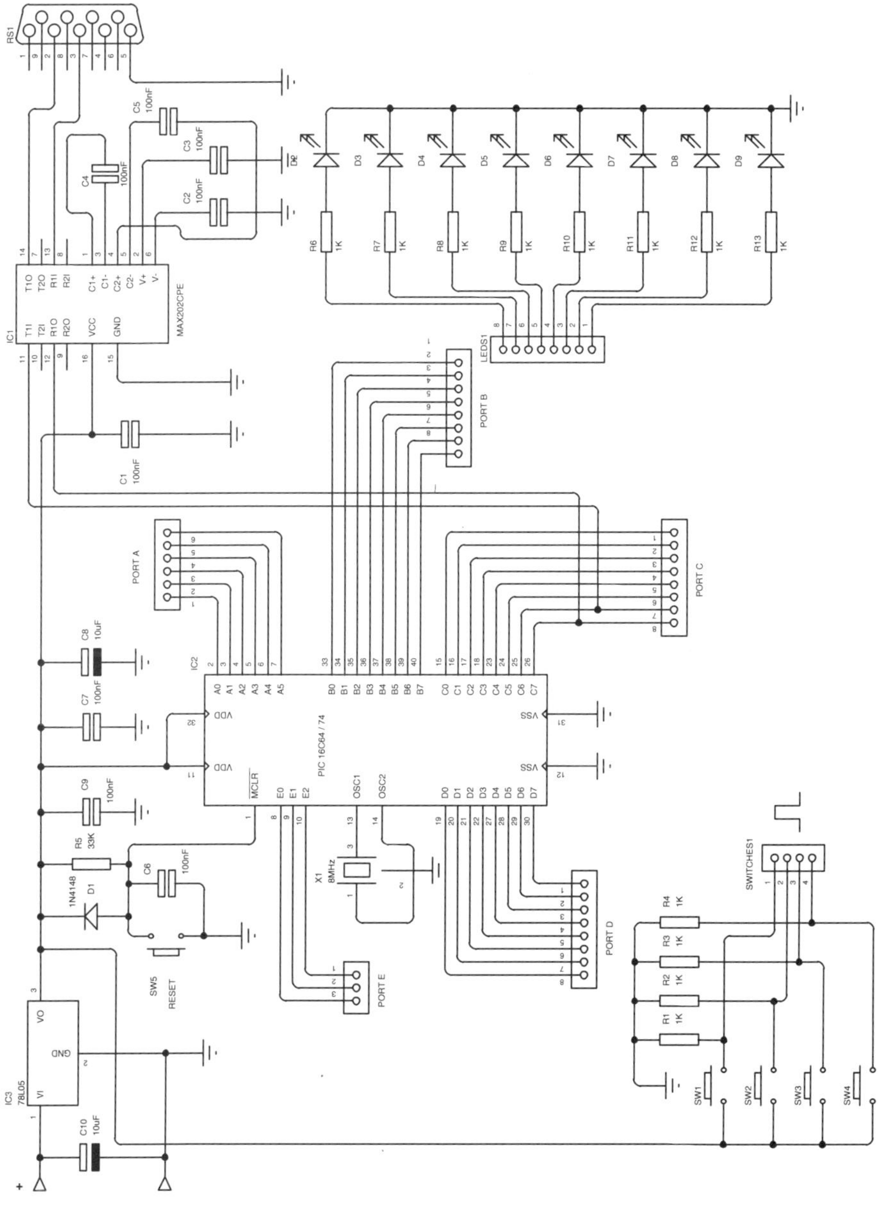

NOTES

C Fundamentals

This chapter presents some of the key aspects of the C programming language. A quick overview of each of these aspects will be given. The goal is to give you a basic knowledge of C so that you can understand the examples in the following chapters.

The topics discussed are:

- **Program structure**
- **Components of a C program**
- **#pragma**
- **Main**
- **#include directive**
- **printf statement**
- **Variables**
- **Constants**
- **Comments**
- **Functions**
- **C keywords**

1

1.1 The Structure of C Programs

All C programs contain preprocessor directives, declarations, definitions, expressions, statements and functions.

Preprocessor directive

A preprocessor directive is a command to the C preprocessor (which is automatically invoked as the first step in compiling a program). The two most common preprocessor directives are the `#define` directive, which substitutes text for the specified identifier, and the `#include` directive, which includes the text of an external file into a program.

Declaration

A declaration establishes the names and attributes of variables, functions and types used in the program. Global variables are declared outside functions and are visible from the end of the declaration to the end of the file. A local variable is declared inside a function and is visible from the end of the declaration to the end of the function.

Definition

A definition establishes the contents of a variable or function. A definition also allocates the storage needed for variables and functions.

Expression

An expression is a combination of operators and operands that yields a single value.

Statement

Statements control the flow or order of program execution in a C program.

1

Function

A function is a collection of declarations, definitions, expressions and statements that performs a specific task. Braces enclose the body of a function. Functions may not be nested in C.

Main Function

All C programs must contain a function named `main` where program execution begins. The braces that enclose the `main` function define the begining and ending point of the program.

Example: General C program structure

```
#include <stdio.h>          /* preprocessor directive */
                            /* include standard C header file */
#define PI  3.142           /* define symbolic constant */

float area;                 /* global declaration */

int square (int r);         /* prototype declaration */

main()
{                           /* beginning of main function */
                            /* and program */
    int radius_squared;     /* local declaration */
    int radius = 3;         /* declaration and initialisation */
    radius_squared = square(radius);    /* pass a value
                                        to a  function */
    area = PI * radius_squared; /* assignment statment */

    printf("Area is %6.4f square units\n",area) ;

}                           /* end of main function & program */

square(int r)               /* function head */
{
    int r_squared;          /* declarations here are known */
                            /* only to square */
```

1

```
    r_squared = r * r;
    return(r_squared);          /* return value to calling */
                                /* statement */
}
```

1.2 Components of a C program

All C programs contain certain essential components such as statements and functions. Statements are the parts of the program that actually perform operations. All C programs contain one or more functions. Functions are subroutines, each of which contains one or more statements and can be called by other parts of the program. When writing programs, indentations, blank lines and comments improve the readability - not only for yourself at a later date, but also for those who bravely follow on. The following example shows some of the required parts of a C program.

```
#include <stdio.h>

/* My 1st C program */

main()
{
    printf("Hello world!");
}
```

The statement `#include <stdio.h>` tells the compiler to include the source code from the file 'stdio.h' into the program.

The extension .h stands for header file. A header file contains information about standard functions that are used in the program. The header file `stdio.h` which is called the **ST**andar**D** **I**nput and **O**utput header file, contains most of the input and output functions. It is necessary to use only the include files that pertain to the standard library functions in your program.

`/* My first C program */` is a comment in C. All comments are preceded by a `/*` and end with a `*/`. Comments are ignored by the compiler and therefore do not affect the speed or length of the compiled code.

All C programs must have a `main()` function. This is the entry point into the program. All functions have the same format which is:

```
FunctionName()
{
code
}
```

Statements within a function are executed sequentially, beginning with the open curly brace and ending with the closed curly brace.

The curly braces { and } show the beginning and end of blocks of code in C.

Finally, the statement `printf("Hello world!");` represents a typical C statement. Almost all C statements end with a semicolon (`;`). The end-of-line character is not recognised by C as a line terminator. Therefore, there are no constraints on the position of statements within a line or the number of statements on a line.

All lines of code have a semi-colon (`;`) at the end to inform the compiler it has reached the end of the statement. Failure to include this will flag an error in the NEXT line. The exception to this is the `if` command where the `;` needs to be at the end of the next line e.g.

```
if (ThisIsTrue)
    DoThisFunction ;
```

1.3 #pragma

The pragma command instructs the compiler to perform a particular action at the compile time such as specifying the PIC being used or the file format generated.

```
#pragma  device  PIC16C54
```

In CCS C the pragma is optional so the following is accepted:

```
#device pic16c54
```

1

1.4 main()

Every program must have a `main` function which can appear only once. No parameters can be placed in the `( )` brackets which follow. As `main` is classed as a function, all code which follows must be placed within a pair of braces `{ }` or curly brackets.

```
main()
{
body of program
}
```

1.5 #include

The header file, (denoted by a .h extension) contains information about library functions such as what argument(s) the function accepts and what argument(s) the function returns or the location of PIC registers for a specific PIC.

```
#include <16C54.h>
```

This information is used by the compiler to link all the hardware specifics and source programs together.

```
#include <16c71.h>
#include <ctype.h>
#use rs232(baud=9600,xmit=PIN_B0,rcv=PIN_B1)

main()
{
    printf("Enter characters: ");
    while(TRUE)
        putc(toupper(getc()));
}
```

The definitions PIN_B0 and PIN_B1 are found in the header file 16C71.H. The function `TOUPPER` is found in the header file CTYPE.H.

Both of these header files must be used in the program so the compiler has essential information about the functions that you are using. Note that many C compilers also require header files for I/O functions like `PRINTF` and `PUTC`. These are built in functions for the PIC that are pulled in via the `#USE RS232` and do not require a separate header file.

Angled brackets

```
#include <thisfile.h>
```

tell the preprocessor to look in predefined include file directories for the file while the quote marks

```
#include "thatfile.h"
```

tell the preprocessor to look in the current directory first.

You have probably noticed that the `#include` directive does not have a semicolon at the end. The reason for this is that the `#include` directive is not a C statement, but instead is a preprocessor directive to the compiler.

The whole of the include file is inserted into the source file at the compile stage.

1.6 printf Function

The `printf` function is a standard library function which allows the programmer to send printable information. The general format for a `printf()` statement is:

```
printf("control_string", argument_list);
```

`control_string` is a string with double quotes at each end. Inside this string any combination of letters, numbers and symbols can be used. Special symbols called format specifiers are denoted with a `%`. The `control_string` must always be present in the `printf()` function. `argument_list` may not be required if there are no format specifiers in the format string. The `argument_list` can be composed of constants and variables. The following two examples show `printf()` statements using a constant and then a variable.

```
printf("Hello world!");

printf("Microchip is #%d!",1);
```

The format specifier (%d) is dependent on the type of data being displayed. The table below shows all of the format specifiers in C and the data types they affect.

Format Specifiers `printf()`

```
%c  single character
%d  signed decimal integer
%f  floating point (decimal notation - must include
    decimal point)
%e  floating point (exponential or scientific notation)
%u  unsigned decimal integer
%x  unsigned hexadecimal integer (lower case)
%X  unsigned hexadecimal integer (upper case)
l   prefix used with %d, %u, %x to specify long integer
```

NOTE a 0 (zero) following a % character within a format string forces leading zeros to be printed out. The number following specifies the width of the printed field.

```
printf("The Hex of decimal 12 is %02x\n",12);
```

would print out

```
The Hex of decimal 12 is 0c
```

Escape Sequences

```
\n  newline
\t  horizontal tab
\r  carriage return
\f  formfeed
\'  single quote
\"  double quote
\\  backslash
%%  percent sign
\?  question mark
\b  backspace
\0  null character
\v  vertical tab
\xhhh   insert HEX code hhh
```

The format specification can also be shown as %[flags][width][.precision] so in a previous example the line:-

```
printf("Area is %6.4f square units\n",area) ;
```

will print out the value area in a field width of 6 with a precision of 4 decimal places.

By default the PRINTF output goes out the last defined RS232 port. The output, however, can be directed to anything defining your own output function. For example:

```
void lcd_putc(char c)
{
    // Insert code to output one
    // character to the LCD here
}
printf(lcd_putc, "value is %u", value);
```

1.7 Variables

A variable is a name for a specific memory location. This memory location can hold various values depending on how the variable was declared. In C, all variables must be declared before they are used. A variables declaration tells the compiler what type of variable is being used. All variable declarations are statements in C and-therefore must be terminated with a semicolon.

The five basic data types that C supports are char, int, float, double, void. The general format for declaring a variable is:

```
type variable_name;
```

An example of declaring a variable is char ch;. The compiler would interpret this statement as the variable ch is declared as a char (8-bit unsigned integer).

1.8 Constants

A constant is a fixed value which cannot be changed by the program. For example, 25 is a constant. Integer constants are specified without any fractional components, such as -100 or 40. Floating point constants require the decimal point followed by the number's fractional component. The number 456.75 is a floating point constant. Character constants are enclosed between single quotes such as 'A' or '&'.

When the compiler encounters a constant in your program, it must decide what type of constant it is. The C compiler will, by default, fit the constant into the smallest compatible data type that will hold it. So 15 is an `int` and 64000 is an `unsigned`.

A constant is declared using the `#define` statement.

```
#define <label> value
```

The `<label>` defines the name you will use throughout your program, **value** is the value you are assigning to `<label>`.

```
#define TRUE 1

#define pi 3.14159265359
```

C allows you to specify constants in hexadecimal and octal formats. Hexadecimal constants must have the prefix '0x'. For example 0xA4 is a valid hexadecimal constant. In addition to numeric constants, C supports string constants. String constants are a set of characters enclosed with double quotes.

Constants defined with `#DEFINE` are textual replacements done before the code is compiled in a stage called pre-processing. Directives that start with # are called pre-processor directives. You can `#DEFINE` any text. For example:

```
#define NOT_OLD (AGE<65)
         .
         .
         .
if NOT_OLD
    printf("YOUNG");
```

`#DEFINE` data is not stored in memory, they are resolved at compile time. To save constants in the chip **ROM**, use **CONST** keyword in a variable declaration. For example:

```
char  CONST  id[5]="1234";
```

1.9 Comments

Comments are used to document the meaning and operation of the source code. All comments are ignored by the compiler. A comment can be placed anywhere in the program except for the middle of a C keyword, function name or variable name. Comments can be many lines long and may also be used to remove temporarily a line of code. Finally, comments cannot be nested.

Comments have two formats. The first format is used by all C compilers and is

```
/* This is a comment */
```

The second format is supported by most compilers and is

```
// This is a comment
```

EXCERCISE Which of the following comments is valid? Invalid?

```
/* My comment is very short */

/* My comment is very, very, very, very, very very, very,
very, very, very, very, very,
very, very, very long and is valid */
/* This comment /* looks */ ok, but is invalid */
```

1.10 Functions

Functions are the basic building blocks of a C program. All C programs contain at least one function, **main()**. Most program that you will write will contain many functions. The format for a C program with many

1

functions is:

```
main()
{
}
    function1()
    {
    }

    function2()
    {
    }
```

`main()` is the first function called when the program is executed. The other functions, `function1()` and `function2()`, can be called by any function in the program.

Traditionally `main()` is not called by any other function, however, there are no restrictions in C.

The following is an example of two functions in C.

```
#include <16C74.h>

main()
{
    printf("I ");
    function1();
    printf("C.");
}
function1()
{
    printf("like ");
}
```

One reminder when writing your own functions is that when the closed curly brace of a function is reached, the program will start executing code one line after the point at which the function was originally called. See also section 3.1.

1.11 MACROS

#DEFINE is a powerful directive as illustrated in the previous section. C allows defines to have parameters making them even more powerful. When parameters are used it is called a macro. Macros are used to enhance readability or to save typing. A simple macro:

```
#define  var(x,v)  unsigned  int  x=v;

var(a,1)
var(b,2)
var(c,3)
```

Is the same as:

```
unsigned int a=1;
unsigned int b=2;
unsigned int c=3;
```

Another example that will be more meaningful after reading the expressions chapter:

```
#define MAX(A,B) ((A>B)?A:B)

z=MAX(x,y);    //  z will contain the larger
value x or y.
```

1.12 Conditional Compilation

C has some special pre-processor directives that allow sections of code to be included or excluded from compilation based on compile time settings. Consider the following example:

```
#define HW_VERSION 5

#if   HW_VERSION>3
    output_high(PIN_B0);
#else
```

```
        output_low(PIN_B0);
    #endif
```

The above will compile only one line depending on the setting of HW_VERSION. There may be dozens of these **#IF's** in a file and the same code could be compiled for different hardware versions just by changing one constant. The **#IF** is evaluated and finished when the code is compiled unlike a normal **IF** that is evaluated when a program runs.

#IFDEF simply checks to see if an ID was **#DEFINED**. Example:

```
#define DEBUG

#ifdef  DEBUG
        printf("ENTERING FUCT X");
#endif
```

In this example all the debugging lines in the program can be eliminated from the compilation by removing the one **#DEFINE** line.

1.13 Hardware Compatibility

The compiler needs to know about the hardware so the code can be compiled correctly. A typical program begins as follows:

```
#include <16c74.h>
#fuses hs,nowdt
#use delay(clock=8000000)
```

The first line included device specific defines such as the pin names. The second line sets the PIC fuses. In this case the high-speed oscillator and no watch dog timer. The last line tells the compiler what the oscillator speed is. The following are some other example lines:

```
#use rs232(baud=9600,xmit=PIN_C6, rcv=PIN_C7)
#use i2c(master,scl=PIN_B6,sda=PIN_B7)
```

In addition C variables may be created and mapped to hardware registers. These variables may be bits or bytes. After they are defined, they may be used in a program like any other variable. Examples:

```
#bit carry=3.0
#byte portb=6
#byte intcon=11
```

1.14 C Keywords

The ANSI C standard defines 32 keywords for use in the C language. In C, certain words are reserved for use by the compiler to define data types or for use in loops. All C keywords must be in lowercase for the compiler to recognise them. Typically, many C compilers will add several additional keywords that take advantage of the processor's architecture.

The following is a list of the keywords which are reserved from use as variable names.

auto	double	int	struct
break	else	long	switch
case	enum	register	typedef
char	extern	return	union
const	float	short	unsigned
continue	for	signed	void
default	goto	sizeof	volatile
do	if	static	while

EXCERCISE

1. Write a program that prints your name to the screen.

2. Write a program that declares one integer variable called year. This variable should be given the value of the current year and then, using a `printf()` statement, display the value of year on the screen. The result of your program should look like this: `The year is 1998`

NOTES

Variables

An important aspect of the C language is how it stores data. This chapter will examine more closely how variables are used in C to store data.

The topics discussed in this chapter are:

data types
declarations
assignments
data type ranges
type conversions

2.1 Data Types

The C programming language supports five basic data types and four type modifiers. The following table shows the meanings of the basic data types and type modifiers.

Type	Meaning	Keyword
character	character data	`char`
integer	signed whole numbers	`int`
float	floating point numbers	`float`
double	double precision floating point numbers	`double`
void	valueless	`void`
signed	positive or negative number	`signed`
unsigned	positive only number	`unsigned`
long	doubles the length of a number	`long`
short	halves the length of a number	`short`

Each of the data types represent a particular range of numbers, which can change depending on the modifier used. The next table shows the possible range of values for all the possible combinations of the basic data types and modifiers.

Type	Bit Width	Range
`short`	1	0 or 1
`short int`	1	0 or 1
`int`	8	0 to 255
`char`	8	0 to 255
`unsigned`	8	0 to 255
`unsigned int`	8	0 to 255
`signed`	8	-128 to 127
`signed int`	8	-128 to 127
`long`	16	0 to 65535
`long int`	16	0 to 65535
`signed long`	16	-32768 to 32767
`float`	32	3.4E-38 to 3.4E+38

NOTE

See individual C compiler documentation for actual data types and numerical range.

C allows a shorthand notation for the data types `unsigned int`, `short int`, and `long int`. Simply use the word `unsigned`, `short`, or `long` without the `int`. To make arithmetic operations easier for the CPU, C represents all negative numbers in the 2's complement format. To find the 2's complement of a number simply invert all the bits and add a 1 to the result. For example, to convert the signed number 29 into 2's complement:


```
00011101 =    29
11100010      invert all bits
       1      add 1
11100011 =    -29
```

Example of assigning a `long` value of 12000 to `a`. 12000 in hex is 2EE0. The following code extract assigns the lower word (E0) to register 11h and the upper word (2E) to 12h

```
long a = 12000;
main()
{
            0007:  MOVLW   E0
            0008:  MOVWF   11
            0009:  MOVLW   2E
            000A:  MOVWF   12
}
```

EXCERCISE

1. Write this statement in another way:
   `long int i;`

2. To understand the difference between a signed number and an unsigned number, type in the following program. The unsigned integer 35000 is represented by -30536 in signed integer format.

```
#include <stdio.h>

main()
{
    int i;                  /* signed integer */
    unsigned int u;         /* unsigned integer */

    u = 35000;
    i = u;
    printf("%d %u\n", i, u);
}
```

2

2.2 Variable Declaration

Variables can be declared in two basic places: inside a function or outside of all functions. The variables are called local and global respectively. Variables are declared in the following manner:

```
type variable_name;
```

where **type** is one of C's valid data types and **variable_name** is the name of the variable.

Local variables (declared inside a function) can only used by statements within the function where they are declared.

The value of a local variable cannot be accessed by functions statements outside of the function. The most important thing to remember about local variables is that they are created upon entry into the function and destroyed when the function is exited. Local variables must also be declared at the start of the function before the statements.

It is acceptable for local variables in different functions to have the same name. Consider the following example.

```
    #include <16C74.h>

void f2(void)
    {
```

```
        int count;
        for (count=0 ; count<10; count++)
        printf("%d \n",count);
    }

f1()
    {
        int count;
        for (count=0; count<10; count++)
             f2();
    }

main()
    {
        f1();
        return 0;
    }
```

This program will print the numbers 0 through 9 on the screen ten times. The operation of the program is not affected by a variable named count located in both functions.

Global variables, on the other hand, can be used by many different functions. Global variables must be declared before any functions that use them. Most importantly, global variables are not destroyed until the execution of the program is complete.

The following example shows how global variables are used.

```
    #include <16C74.h>
    int max;

    f1()
    {
        int i;
        for(i=0; i<max; i++)
        printf("%d ",i);

    }

    main()
    {
```

```
        max = 10;
        f1();
        return 0;
    }
```


In this example, both functions `main()` and `f1()` reference the variable `max`. The function `main()` assigns a value to max and the function `f1()` uses the value of max to control the `for` loop.

EXCERCISE⇨

1. What are the main differences between local and global variables?
2. Both local and global variables may share the same name in C. Type in the following program.

```
#include <stdio.h>

int count;

f1()
{
    int count;
    count=100;
    printf(″count in f1(): %d\n″,count);
}

main()
{
    count=10;
    f1();
    printf(″count in main(): %d\n″,count);
    return 0;
}
```

In `main()` the reference to `count` is the global variable. In `f1()` the local variable `count` overrides the usage of the global variable.

2.3 Variable Assignment

Up to now we have only discussed how to declare a variable in a program and not really how to assign a value to it. Assignment of values to variables is simple:

```
variable_name = value ;
```

Since a variable assignment is a statement, we have to include the semicolon at the end. An example of assigning the value 100 to the integer variable count is:

```
count = 100 ;
```

The value 100 is called a constant.

Variables values can be initialized at the same time as they are declared. This makes it easier and more reliable in setting the starting values in you program to known conditions. Eg

```
int  a = 10, b = 0, c = 0x23;
```

Many different types of constants exist in C. A character constant is specified by enclosing the character in single quotes, such as `'M'`. Whole numbers are used when assigning values to integers. Floating point numbers must use a value with a decimal point. For example, to tell C that the value 100 is a floating point value, use `100.0`.

A variable can also be assigned the value of another variable. The following program illustrates this assignment.

```
main()
{
    int i;
    int j;

    i=0;
    j=i;
}
```

EXCERCISE

1. Write a program that declares one integer variable called **count**. Give **count** a value of **100** and use a **printf()** statement to display the value. The output should look like this:

```
100 is the value of count
```

2

2. Write a program that declares three variables, **char, float,** and **double** with variable names of **ch, f,** and **d.** Assign a **'R'** to the char, **50.5** to the float, and **156.007** to the double. Display the value of these variables to the screen. The output should look like this:

```
ch is R
f is 50.5
d is 156.007
```

2.4 Enumeration

In C, it is possible to create a list of named integer constants. This declaration is called enumeration. The list of constants created with an enumeration can be used any place an integer can be used. The general form for creating an enumeration is:

```
enum name {enumeration list} variable(s);
```

The variable list is an optional item of an enumeration. Enumeration variables may contain only the values that are defined in the enumeration list. For example, in the statement

```
enum color_type {red,green,yellow} color;
```

the variable **color** can only be assigned the values **red, green** or **yellow. i.e. color = red;**

The compiler will assign integer values to the enumeration list starting with 0 at the first entry. Each entry is one greater than the previous one. Therefore, in the above example **red** is **0**, **green** is **1** and **yellow** is **2**. This default value can be overridden by specifying a value for a constant. This example illustrates this technique.

```
enum color_type {red,green=9,yellow} color;
```

This statement assigns **0** to **red, 9** to **green** and **10** to **yellow.**

Once an enumeration is defined, the name can be used to create additional variables at other points in the program. For example, the variable **mycolor** can be created with the **colortype** enumeration by:

```
enum color_type mycolor;
```

The variable can also be tested against another one, i.e.

```
if (color==fruit)
// do something
```

Essentially, enumeration's help to document code, instead of assigning a value to a variable and enumeration can be used to clarify the meaning of the value.

EXCERCISE⇨

1. Create an enumeration of the PICl7CXX family line.
2. Create an enumeration of currency from the lowest to highest denomination.
3. Is the following fragment correct? Why/Why not?

```
enum {PIC16C51,PIC16C52,PIC16C53} device;
    device = PIC16C52;
    printf("First PIC was %s\n",device);
```

2.5 typedef

The **typedef** statement is used to create a new name for an existing type. The format is:

```
typedef old_name new_name;
```

The new name can be used to declare variables. For instance, the following program uses the name `smallint` for the type signed `char`.


```
#include <16C74.h>

typedef signed char smallint;

main()
{
    smallint i;
    for(i=0;i<10;i++)
        printf("%d ",i);
  }
```

When using `typedefs`, you must remember two key points. Firstly, a `typedef` does not deactivate the original name or type. In the previous example, `signed char` is still a valid type. Secondly, several `typedef` statements can be used to create many new names for the same original type.

`Typedefs` are typically used for two reasons. The first is to create portable programs. If the program you are writing will be used on machines with 16-bit and 32-bit integers, you might want to ensure that only 16-bit integers are used. The program for 16-bit integers would use

```
typedef int myint;
```

to make all integers declared as `myint` 16-bits. Then, before compiling the program for the 32-bit computer, the `typedef` statement should be changed to

```
typedef short int myint;
```

so that all integers declared as `myint` are 16-bits.

The second reason to use `typedef` statements is to help you document your code. If your code contains many variables used to hold a count of some sort, you could use the following `typedef` statement to declare all your `counter` variables

```
typedef int counter;
```

Someone reading your code would recognise that any variable declared as **`counter`** is used as a counter in the program.

EXCERCISE⇨

1. Make a new name for **`unsigned long`** called UL. Use this **`typedef`** in a short program that declares a variable using UL, assigns a value to it and displays the value to the screen.
2. Is the following segment of code valid?

```
typedef int height;
typedef height length;
typedef length depth;

depth d;
```

2.6 type Conversions

C allows you to mix different data types together in one expression. For example, the following is a valid code fragment:

```
char ch = '0';
int i = 15;
float f = 25.6;
```

The mixing of data types is governed by a strict set of conversion rules that tell the compiler how to resolve the differences. The first part of the rule set is a type promotion. The C compiler will automatically promote a **`char`** or **`short int`** in an expression to an **`int`** when the expression is evaluated. A type promotion is only valid during the evaluation of the expression, the variable itself does not become physically larger.

Now that the automatic type promotions have been completed, the C compiler will convert all variables in the expression up to the type of the largest variable. This task is done on an operation by operation basis.

The following algorithm shows the type conversions:

IF an operand is a long double
THEN the second is converted to long double
ELSE IF an operand is a double
THEN the second is converted to double
ELSE IF an operand is a float
THEN the second is converted to float
ELSE IF an operand is an unsigned long
THEN the second is converted to unsigned long
ELSE IF an operand is long
THEN the second is converted to long
ELSE IF an operand is unsigned
THEN the second is converted to unsigned

Let's take a look at the previous example and discover what type of promotions and conversions are taking place. First of all, `ch` is promoted to an `int`. The first operation is the multiplication of `ch` with `i`. Since both of these variables are now integers, no type conversion takes place. The next operation is the division between `ch*i` and `f`. The algorithm specifies that if one of the operands is a float, the other will be converted to a float. The result of `ch* i` will be converted to a floating point number then divided by `f`. Finally, the value of the expression `ch*i/f` is a float, but will be converted to a double for storage in the variable `result`.

Instead of relying on the compiler to make the type conversions, you can specify the type conversion by using the following format:

```
(type) value
```

This is called type casting. This causes a temporary change in the variable. `type` is a valid C data type and `value` is the variable or constant. The following code fragment shows how to print the integer portion of a floating point number.

```
float f;

f = 100.2;
```

```
printf("%d",(int)f);
```

The number `100` will be printed to the screen after the segment of code is executed.

If two 8-bit integers are multiplied, the result will be an 8-bit value. If the resulting value is assigned to a long, the result will still be an 8-bit integer as the arithmetic is performed before the result is assigned to the new variable.

```
Ie  int a = 250, b = 10;
    long c;
    c = a * b;
```

the result will be 196

So If you need a long value as the answer, then at least one value needs to be initially defined as long or typecast.

```
c = (long) a * b;
```

the result will be 2500 because `a` was first typecast to a `long` and therefore a long multiply was done.

2.7 variable storage class

Every variable and function in C has two attributes - type and storage class. The type has already been discussed `char, int` etc. There are four storage classes - automatic, external, static and register and have the following C names -

```
auto   extern  static  register
```

Auto

Variables declared within a function are auto by default, so

```
{   char c;
```

```
        int a, b, e;
    }
```

is the same as

```
    {   autocharc;
        autoint a, b, e;
    }
```

When a block of code is entered, the compiler assigns RAM space for the declared variables. The RAM locations are used in that 'local' block of code and can / will be used by other blocks of code.

```
    main()
    {   char c = 0;
        int  a = 1, b = 3, e = 5;
            0007:  CLRF    0E    - register 0Eh assigned
                                   to C
            0008:  MOVLW   01    - load w with 1
            0009:  MOVWF   0F    - load register assigned
                                   to a with w
            000A:  MOVLW   03    - load w with 3
            000B:  MOVWF   10    - load register assigned
                                   to b with w
            000C:  MOVLW   05    - load w with 5
            000D:  MOVWF   11    - load register assigned
                                   to e with w
    }
```

Extern

All functions and variables declared outside a function body have a storage class set as external. The RAM locations are permanently assigned to the variable and are shared throughout the program by all functions - no function within the CCS C.

Static

The variable class **static** defines globally active variables which are initialized to zero unless otherwise defined.

```
void test()
{
    charx,y,z;
    static int  count = 4;
    printf("count = %d\n",++count);
}
```

The variable **count** is initialised once and thereafter increments every time the function test is called.

Register

The variable class register originates from large system applications where it would be used to reserve high speed memory for frequently used variables. The class is used only to advise the compiler - no function within the CCS C.

NOTES

Functions

Functions are the basic building blocks of the C language. All statements must be within functions. In this chapter we will discuss how to pass arguments to functions and how to receive an argument from a function.

The topics discussed in this chapter are:

Passing Arguments to Functions
Returning Arguments from Functions
Function Prototypes
Classic and Modern Function Declarations

3.1 Functions

In previous sections, we have seen many instances of functions being called from a main program. For instance:

```
main()
{
     f1();
}

f1()
{
return1;
}
```

In reality, this program should produce an error or, at the very least, a warning. The reason is that the function **f1()** must be declared or defined before it is used, just like variables. If you are using a standard C function, the header file that you included at the top of your program has already informed the compiler about the function. If you are using one of your functions, there are two ways to correct this error. One is to use function prototypes which are explained in the next section. The other is to reorganise your program like this:

```
f1()
{
return1;
}

main()
{
     f1();
}
```

An error will not be generated because the **function f1()** is defined before it is called in **main().**

3.2 Function Prototypes

There are two methods to inform the compiler what type of value a function returns. The general form is:

```
type function_name();
```

For instance, the statement `int sum()` would tell the compiler that the function `sum()` returns an integer. The second way to inform the compiler about the return value of a function is the function prototype. A function prototype not only gives the return value of the function, but also declares the number and type of arguments that the function accepts. The prototype must match the function declaration exactly.

Prototypes help the programmer to identify bugs in the program by reporting any illegal type conversions between the arguments passed to a function and the function declaration. It also reports if the number of arguments sent to a function is not the same as specified in the function declaration.

The general format for a function prototype is shown here:

```
type function_name(type var1, type var2, type var3);
```

In the above example, the type of each variable can be different. An example of a function prototype is shown in this program. The function calculates the volume defined by length, width and height.

```
#include <16C74.h>

int volume(int s1, int s2, int s3);

void main()
{
    int vol;
    vol = volume(5,7,12);
    printf("volume: %d\n",vol);
}
```

```
int volume(int s1, int s2, int s3)
{
    return s1*s2*s3;
}
```

Notice that the return uses an expression instead of a constant or variable.

The importance of prototypes may not be apparent with the small programs that we have been doing up to now. However, as the size of programs grows from a few lines to many thousands of lines, the importance of prototypes in debugging errors is evident.

EXCERCISE

1. To show how errors are caught by the compiler, change the above program to send four parameters to the function volume, i.e. `vol = volume(5,7,12,15)`

2. Is the following program correct? Why/Why not?

```
#include <16C74.h>

double myfunc();

void main(void)
{
    printf("%f\n",myfunc(10.2));
}

double myfunc(double num)
{
    return num/2.0;
}
```

3.3 Void

One exception is when a function does not have any parameters passed in or out. This function would be declared as such: `void nothing (void)`.

An example of this could be:-

```
#include <16C74.h>

double pi(void)          // defining the function
{                        // with nothing passed in
return 3.1415926536 ;    // but with pi returned
}

main()
{
     double pi_val;
     pi_val = pi();      // calling the value of pi
     printf("%d\n",pi_val);
}
```


3.4 Using Function Arguments

A function argument is a value that is passed to the function when the function is called. C allows from zero to several arguments to be passed to functions. The number of arguments that a function can accept is compiler dependent, but the ANSI C standard specifies that a function must be able to accept at least 31 arguments.

When a function is defined, special variables must be declared to receive parameters. These special variables are defined as formal parameters. The parameters are declared between the parenthesis that follow the function's name. For example, the function below calculates and prints the sum of two integers that are sent to the function when it is called.

```
sum(int a, int b)
{
    printf("%d\n", a+b);
}
```

An example of how the function would be called in a program is:

```
#include <stdio.h>
```

```
void sum(int a,int b);    // This is a function prototype

main()
{
     sum(1,10);
     sum(15,6);
     sum(100,25);
}

void sum(int a, int b)
{
     printf("%d\n", a+b);
}
```


When **sum()** is called, the compiler will copy the value of each argument into the variables **a** and **b**. It is important to remember that the values passed to the function **(1,10,15,6,100,25)** are called arguments and the variables **a** and **b** are the formal parameters.

Functions can pass arguments in two ways. The first way is called "call by value". This method copies the value of an argument into the formal parameter of the function. Any changes made to the formal parameter do not affect the original value of the calling routine. The second method is called "call by reference". In this method, the address of the argument is copied into the formal parameter of the function. Inside this function, the formal parameter is used to access the actual variable in the calling routine. This means that changes can be made to the variable by using the formal parameter. We will discuss this further in the chapter on pointers. For now, we will only use the call by value method when we pass arguments to a function.

You might have noticed that when the program is compiled a warning message about a missing prototype for the function **sum()** appears. Don't worry about this message now, we will cover how to prototype a function later in this chapter.

EXCERCISE

1. Write a function that takes an integer argument and prints the value to the screen.
2. What is wrong with this program?

```
#include <stdio.h>

print_it(int num)
{
    printf("%d\n",num);
}

main()
{
    print_it(156.7);
}
```

3.5 Using Functions to Return Values

Any function in C can return a value to the calling routine. Typically, the function is put on the right side of an equals sign. The return value does not necessarily need to be used in an assignment statement, but could be used in a `printf()` statement. The general format for telling the compiler that a function returns a value is:

```
type function_name(formal parameters)
{
    <statements>
    return value;
}
```

where type specifies the data type of the return value of the function. A function can return any data type except an array. If no data type is specified, then the C compiler assumes that the function is returning an integer `(int)`. If your function does not return a value, the ANSI C standard specifies that the function should return void. This explicitly tells the compiler that the function does not return a value.

This example shows a typical usage for a function that has a return value.

```
#include <16C74.h>
#include <math.h>

main()
{
    double result;
    result = sqrt(16.0);
    printf ("%f\n", result);
}
```

This program calls the function **sqrt()** which returns a floating point number. This number is assigned to the variable **result**. Notice that the header file **math.h** is included because it contains information about **sqrt()** that is used by the compiler.

It is important that you match the data type of the return value of the function to the data type of the variable to which it will be assigned. The same goes for the arguments that you send to a function.

So, how do you return a value from a function? The general form is:

```
return variable_name;
```

where **variable_name** is a constant, variable or any valid C expression that has the same data type as the return value. The following example shows both type of functions.

```
    main()
{
    int num;
    num = func();
    printf ("%d\n", num);
    num = sum(5,127);
    printf ("%d\n", num);
}

func()
{
```

```
    return 6;
}


sum(int a, int b)
{
    int result;

    result = a + b;
    return result;
}
```


One important thing to note is that when a return statement is encountered, the function returns immediately to the calling routine. Any statements after the return will not be executed. The return value of a function is not required to be assigned to a variable or to be used in an expression, however, if it is not then the value is lost.

EXCERCISE⇨

1. Write a function that accepts an integer number between 1 and 100 and returns the square of that number.

2. What is wrong with this function?

```
#include <16C74.h>


main()
{
    double result;
    result = f1();
    printf ("%f\n",result);
}

int f1()
{
    return 60;
}
```

3.6 Classic and Modern Function Declarations

The original version of C used a different method of formal parameter declaration. This form, now called the classic form, is shown below:

```
type function_name(var1,var2,..,varn)
type var1;
type var2;
     .
     .
type varn;
{
     <statements>
}
```

Notice that the declaration is divided into two parts. Only the names of parameters are included inside the parenthesis. Outside of the parenthesis the data types and formal parameter names are specified.

The modern form, which we have been using in previous examples, is given by:

```
type function_name(type parameter1,...,
type parametern)
```

In this type of function declaration, both the data types and formal parameter names are specified between the parenthesis.

The ANSI C standard allows for both type of function declarations. The reason is to maintain compatibility with older C programs of which there are literally billions of lines of C code. If you see the classic form in a piece of code, don't worry, your C compiler should be able to handle it. Going forward, you should use the modern form when writing code.

EXCERCISE

1 What is a function prototype and what are the benefits of using it ?
2 Convert this program using a classical form for the function declarations to the modern form.

```
#include <16C74.h>

void main(void)
{
    printf("area = %d\n", area(10,15));
}

area(l,w)
int l,w;
{
    return l*w;
}
```


3.7 Passing Constant Strings

Because the PIC has limitations on ROM access, constant strings can not be passed to functions in the ordinary manner.

The CCS C compiler handles this situation in a non-standard manner. If a constant string is passed to a function that allows only a character parameter then the function is called for every character in the string. For example:

```
void lcd_putc(char c){
    .   .   .
}

lcd_putc("abcd");

Is the same as:

lcd_putc('a');
```

```
lcd_putc('b');
lcd_putc('c');
lcd_putc('d');
```

C Operators

In C, the expression plays an important role. The main reason is that C defines more operators than most other languages. An expression is a combination of operators and operands. In most cases, C operators follow the rules of algebra and should look familiar.

In this chapter we will discuss many different types of operators including:-

Arithmetic
Relational
Logical
Bitwise
Increment and Decrement
Precedence of Operators

4.1 Arithmetic Operators

The C language defines five arithmetic operators for addition, subtraction, multiplication, division and modulus.

```
+    addition
-    subtraction
*    multiplication
/    division
%    modulus
```

The **+, - , *,** and / operators may be used with any data type. The modulus operator, %, can be used only with integers. The modulus operator gives the remainder of an integer division. Therefore, this operator has no meaning when applied to a floating point number.

The - operator can be used two ways, the first being a subtraction operator. The second is used to reverse the sign of a number. The following example illustrates the two uses of the - sign.

```
a = a - b        ;    subtraction
a = -a           ;    reversing the sign of a
```

Arithmetic operators can be used with any combination of constants and/or variables. For example, the following expression is a valid C statement.

```
result = count - 163;
```

C also gives you some shortcuts when using arithmetic operators. One of the previous examples, **a = a - b**;, can also be written **a -= b;.** This method can be used with the **+, -, *,** and / operators. The example shows various ways of implementing this method.

```
            is the same as
a*=b              a=a*b
a/=b              a=a/b
a+=b              a=a+b
a-=b              a=a-b
```

```
a%=b                a=a%b
a<<=b               a=a<<b
a>>=b               a=a>>b
a&=b                a=a&b
a|=b                a=a|b
a^=b                a=a^b
```

Taking the C code and comparing it to the assembled version shows how the arithmetic function is achieved within the PIC.

```
int a,b,c;
a = b + c;
      becomes
      0007:  MOVF    0F,W  ; load b
      0008:  ADDWF   10,W  ; add c to b
      0009:  MOVWF   0E    ; save in a

a = b - c;
      becomes
      0007:  MOVF    0F,W  ; load b
      0008:  MOVWF   0E    ; save in a
      0009:  MOVF    10,W  ; load c
      000A:  SUBWF   0E,F  ; subtract from a
```

The importance of understanding assembler becomes apparant when dealing with problems - I have found at times that looking at the assembler listing (.LST) points to the C error. One simple fault is the use of = or ==.

```
a = b;
      becomes
      0007:  MOVF    0F,W  ; load b
      0008:  MOVWF   0E    ; save in a
while
a==b;
      becomes
      0007:  MOVF    0F,W  ; load b
      0008:  SUBWF   0E,W  ; subtract from a
      0009:  BTFSC   03,2  ; test if zero
      000A:  GOTO    00D   ; yes - so bypass
```

In the first instance, `a` is made the same as `b`, in the second, `a` is tested to check if it is the same as `b`.

EXCERCISE⇨

1. Write a program that finds the remainder of 5/5, 5/4, 5/3, 5/2, and 5/1.
2. Write a program that calculates the number of seconds in a year.

4.2 Relational Operators

The relational operators in C compare two values and return a true or false result based on the comparison. The relational operators are

```
>    greater than
>=   greater than or equal to
<    less than
<=   less than or equal to
==   equal to
!=   not equal to
```

One thing to note about relational operators is that the result of a comparison is always a 0 or 1, even though C defines true as any non-zero value. False is always defined as zero.

The following examples show some expressions with relational operators.

```
var > 15  if var is less than or equal to 15, the
result is 0 (false)
var != 15 if var is greater or less than 15, the
result is 1 (true)
```

EXCERCISE⇨

1. Rewrite the following expression using a different relational operator.

```
count != 0
```

2. When is this expression true or false? Why?

```
count >= 35
```

4.3 Logical Operators

The logical operators support the basic logical operations AND, OR, and NOT. Again, these operators return either a 0 for false or 1 for true. The logical operators and truth table for these operators is shown here:

<table>
<tr><td></td><td></td><td>AND</td><td>OR</td><td>NOT</td></tr>
<tr><td>p</td><td>q</td><td>p&&q</td><td>p||p</td><td>!p</td></tr>
<tr><td>0</td><td>0</td><td>0</td><td>0</td><td>1</td></tr>
<tr><td>0</td><td>1</td><td>0</td><td>1</td><td>1</td></tr>
<tr><td>1</td><td>0</td><td>0</td><td>1</td><td>0</td></tr>
<tr><td>1</td><td>1</td><td>1</td><td>1</td><td>0</td></tr>
</table>

The logical and relational operators are tightly coupled together when evaluating an expression. An example of linking these operators together is:

```
count>max || !(max==57) && var>=0
```

Another part of C that uses the relational and logical operators is the program control statements that we will cover in the next chapter.

EXCERCISE

1. Rewrite the following expressions using any combination of relational and logical operators.

```
count == 0

result <= 5
```

2. Since C does not explicitly provide for an exclusive OR function, write an XOR function based on the following truth table.

p	q	XOR
0	0	0
0	1	1
1	0	1
1	1	0

4.4 Bitwise Operators

C contains six special operators which perform bit-by-bit operations on numbers. These bitwise operators can be used only on integer and character data types. The result of using any of these operators is a bitwise operation of the operands. The bit-wise operators are:

```
&    bitwise AND
|    bitwise OR
^    bitwise XOR
~    1's complement
>>   right shift
<<   left shift
```

The general format for using the shift operators is:

```
variable << expression

variable >> expression
```

The value of expression determines how many places to the left or right the variable is shifted. Each left shift causes all bits to shift one bit position to the left and a zero is inserted on the right side. The bit that is shifted off the end of the variable is lost.

The unique thing to note about using left and right shifts is that a left shift is equivalent to multiplying a number by 2 and a right shift is equivalent to dividing a number by 2. Shift operations are almost always faster than the equivalent arithmetic operation due to the way a CPU works.

An example of all the bitwise operators is shown.

```
    AND                                 OR
    000000101    (5)                    00000101     (5)
&   000000110    (6)          |         00000110     (6)
    000000100    (4)                    00000111     (7)

    XOR                                 NOT (ones compliment)
    00000101(5)          ~              00000101     (5)
^   00000110(6)                         11111010     (250)
    00000011(3)

    LEFT SHIFT                          RIGHT SHIFT
    00000101     (5)                    00000101     (5)
    <<  2                               >>  2
=   00010100(20)                        00000001     (1)
```

NOTE do not shift by more bits than the operand has - undefined result


```
a = b | c;
```

becomes

```
0007:   MOVF    0F,W   ; load b
0008:   IORWF   10,W   ; inclusive or with c
0009:   MOVWF   0E; save in a
```

```
a = b & c;
```

becomes

```
0007:   MOVF    0F,W   ; load b
0008:   ANDWF   10,W   ; and function with c
0009:   MOVWF   0E; save in a
```

```
a = b>>3
```

becomes

```
0007:   MOVF    0F,W   ; load b into w
0008:   MOVWF   0E; save it in b
0009:   RRF     0E,F   ; rotate contents
000A:   RRF     0E,F   ; right
000B:   RRF     0E,F   ; three times
000C:   MOVLW   1F; apply mask to contents
000D:   ANDWF   0E,F   ; of register for b
```

```
j = ~a;
```

becomes

```
0009:  MOVF    0F,W     ; load a
000A:  MOVWF   0E       ; save in j
000B:  COMF    0E,F     ; compliment j
```

Mixing it all together

Written	Operation
`sum = a+b++`	`sum = a+b` `b = b+1`
`sum = a+b–`	`sum = a+b` `b = b-1`
`sum = a+ ++b`	`b = b+1` `sum = a+b`
`sum = a+ –b`	`b = b-1` `sum = a+b`

EXCERCISE

1. Write a program that inverts only the MSB of a signed char.
2. Write a program that displays the binary representation of a number with the data type of char.

4.5 Increment and Decrement Operators

How would you increment or decrement a variable by one? Probably one of two statements pops into your mind. Maybe `a = a+1;` or `a = a-1;`

Again, the makers of C have come up with a shorthand notation for increment or decrement of a number. The general formats are:

```
a++ or  ++a for increment
a–  or  –a  for decrement
```

When the ++ or – sign precedes the variable, the variable is incremented then that value is used in an expression. When the ++ or – follows the variable, the value of the variable is used in the expression then incremented.

```
int j, a = 3;
    0007:   MOVLW   03
    0008:   MOVWF   0F     ; register assigned to a

j = ++a;
    0009:   INCF    0F,F   ; a = 4
    000A:   MOVF    0F,W   ; j = 4
    000B:   MOVWF   0E     ; register assigned to j

j = a++;
    000C:   MOVF    0F,W   ; load value of a into w
    000D:   INCF    0F,F   ; a = 5
    000E:   MOVWF   0E     ; j = 4
```


NOTE Do not use the format

```
a = a++;
```

as the following code will be generated

```
MOVF    0E,W     ; value of a loaded into w
INCF    0E,F     ; value in a incremented
MOVWF   0E       ; previous value reloaded overwriting
                   incremented value
```

The following example illustrates the two uses.

```
#include <16C74.h>

void main (void)
{
    int i,j;

    i = 10;
    j = i++;
    printf("i = %d, j = %d\n",i,j);
```

```
        i = 10;
        j = ++i;
        printf("i = %d, j = %d\n",i,j);
    }
```

The first `printf()` statement will print an `11` for `i` and a `10` for `j`. The second `printf()` statement will print an `11` for both `i` and `j`.

EXCERCISE⇨

1. Rewrite the assignment operations in this program to increment or decrement statements.


```
#include <16C74.h>

void main (void)
{
  int a, b;

  a = 1;
  a = a+1;
  b = a;
  b = b-1;
  printf("a=%d, b=%d\n", a, b);
}
```

2. What are the values of `a` and `b` after this segment of code finishes executing?

```
a = 0;
b = 0;
a = ++a + b++;
a++;
b++;
b = —a + ++b;
```

4.6 Precedence of operators

Precedence refers to the order in which operators are processed by the C compiler. For instance, if the expression `a+b*c` was encountered in your program, which operation would happen first? Addition or multiplication? The C language maintains a precedence for all operators. The following shows the precedence from highest to lowest.

Priority	Operator	Example	
1	()	(a+b)/c	parenthesis
2	! ~ ++ — - * & sizeof	a=&b	plus/minus/NOT/compliment increment/decrement/sizeof
3	* / %	a%b	multiply/divide/modulus
4	+ -	a+b	add/subtract
5	« »	a=b>>c	shift left or right
6	< <= > >=	a>=b	greater/less/equal than
7	== != &	a=b&c	bitwise AND
8	|	a=b|c	bitwise OR
9	^	a=b^c	bitwise XOR
10	&&	a&&b	logical AND
11	||	a||b	logical OR
12	= += -= *= /=	a=b	assignment

Some of these operators we have not yet covered, but don't worry, they will be covered later. The second line is composed entirely of unary operators such as increment and decrement. Parenthesis can be used to set the specific order in which operations are performed.

A couple of examples of using parenthesis to clarify or change the precedence of a statement are:

```
10-2*5 = 0
(10-2)*5 = 40
count*num+88/val-19%count
(count*num) + (88/val) - (19%count)
```

EXCERCISE

1. What are the values of `a` and `b` after this segment of code finishes executing?

```
int a=0,b=0;

a = 6*8+3*b++;
b += —a*2+3*4;
```

NOTES

C Program Control Statements

In this chapter you will learn about the statements that C uses to control the flow of execution in your program. You will also learn how relational and logical operators are used with these control statements. We will also cover how to execute loops.

Topics discussed in this chapter include:

- **if**
- **if-else**
- **for**
- **while**
- **do-while**
- **nesting loops**
- **break**
- **continue**
- **switch**
- **null**
- **return**

5.1 if Statement

The `if` statement is a conditional statement. The block of code associated with the `if` statement is executed based upon the outcome of a condition. Again, any non-zero value is true and any zero value is false. The simplest format is:

```
if (expression)
     statement;
```

NOTE no ;

The expression can be any valid C expression. The `if` statement evaluates the expression which has a result of true or false. If the expression is true, the statement is executed. If the expression is false, the program continues without executing the statement. A simple example of an `if` is:

```
if(num > 0)
     printf("The number is positive\n");
```


This example shows how relational operators are used with program control statements.

The `if` statement can also be used to control the execution of blocks of code. The general format is:

```
if (expression)
{
.
statement;
.
}
```

The braces { and } are used to enclose the block of code. This tells the compiler that if the expression is true, execute the code between the braces.

An example of the `if` and a block of code is:

```
if (count < 0)
{
    count = 0;
    printf ("Count down\n");
}
```

or

```
if(TestMode == 1)
    {
    ..... print parameters to user
    }
```

Other Operator comparisons used in the **if** statement are :-

```
x == y      x equals y
x != y      x is not equal to y
x > y       x greater than y
x < y       x less than y
x <= y      x less than or equal to y
x >= y      x greater than or equal to y
x && y      logical AND
x || y      logical OR
```

An example of one such function - converted into assembler is:

```
int j, a = 3;

    0007:  MOVLW   03    ; load a with 3
    0008:  MOVWF   0F

if (j == 2)

    0009:  MOVLW   02    ; load j with 2
    000A:  SUBWF   0E,W  ; test for match
    000B:  BTFSS   03,2  ; ie zero
    000C:  GOTO    00F
{
j = a;

    000D:  MOVF    0F,W  ; if zero then
    000E:  MOVWF   0E    ; load a into j
```

EXCERCISE⇨

1. Which of these expressions results in a true value?

```
a.  0
b.  1
```

```
c.   -1
d.   5*5<25
e.   1==1
```

2. Write a function that tells whether a number is even or odd. The function returns 0 when the number is even and 1 when the number is odd. Call this function with the numbers 1 and 2.

5.2 if-else Statements

What if you have two blocks of code that are executed based on the outcome of an expression? If the expression is true, the first block of code is executed, if the expression is false the second block of code is executed. You would probably use the `if` statement combined with an `else` statement. The general format for an `if-else` statement is:

```
if (expression)
     statement1;
else
     statement2;
```


The format for an `if-else` statement that uses blocks of code (more than one line) is:

```
if (expression)
     {
     .
     statement;
     .
     }
else
     {
     .
     statement;
     .
     }
```

Keep in mind that an `if` or `else` statement can have as many statements as needed. The curly braces can be thrown away when there is only one statement for the `if` or `else`. An example of a single statement `if-else` is:

```
if (num<0)
    printf("Number is negative.\n");
else
    printf("Number is positive.\n");
```

The addition of the `else` statement provides a two-way decision path for you. But what if you wanted to combine many `if` and `else` statements together to make many decisions? What a coincidence, C provides a method by which you can combine `if's` with `else's` to provide many levels of decision. The general format is:

```
if (expression1)
    {
    statement(s)
    }
else if(expression2)
    {
    statement(s)
    }
else
    {
    statement(s)
    }
```

Here we see that many different expressions can be evaluated to pick a block of code to execute. Rather than explain any more about this method, here is a simple example.

```
if(num == 1)
    printf("got 1\n");
else if(num == 2)
    printf("got 2\n");
else if(num == 3)
    printf("got 3\n");
else
    printf ("got nothing\n");
```

NOTE Within the if statement, care must be made to ensure correct use of the single and double comparison i.e. a single &, = or | has the effect of causing the function to act upon the variable as opposed to the double &&, == or || which acts as a comparison of the variable under test. This is a common mistake and may not be immediately apparent as code will compile but will fail in operation.

EXCERCISE⇨

1. Is this fragment of code correct?

```
if (count>20)

        printf("count is greater than 20");
        count— ;
}
```

2. Write a program that prints either pence, 5 pence, 10 pence, 20 pence, 50 pence or a pound depending on the value of the variable. The only valid values for the variable are 1, 5, 10, 25, 50 and 100

5.3 ? Operator

The `?` operator is actually a shorthand notation of the `if else` statement. The format is:

```
(expr1) ? (expr2) : (expr3);
```

where each of the `expr?` is a valid C statement. First, `expr1` is evaluated. If the result is TRUE (remember that this is any non-zero value), then `expr2` is evaluated. If the result is FALSE (zero), then `expr3` is evaluated. The following is an example of the `?` operator.

```
int i,j;
i = 1;
i ? j=0 : j=1;
```

Since `i` is 1 or non-zero, the expression `j=0` will be evaluated.

Unlike an **IF** statement the **?** operator returns a value. For example:

```
i = (i<20) ?  i+1 : 10;
```

i will be incremented unless it is 20 or higher then it is assigned 10.

5.4 for Loop

One of the three loop statements that C provides is the **for** loop. If you have a statement or set of statements that needs to be repeated, a **for** loop easily implements this. The basic format of a **for** loop is similar to that of other languages such as BASIC or Pascal. The most common form of a **for** loop is:

```
for( initialization ; conditional_test ; increment )
```

The **initialization** section is used to give an initial value to the loop counter variable. Note that this counter variable must be declared before the **for** loop can use it. This section of the **for** loop is executed only once. The **conditional_test** is evaluated prior to each execution of the loop. Normally this section tests the loop counter variable for a true or false condition. If the **conditional_test** is true the loop is executed. If the **conditional_test** is false the loop exits and the program proceeds. The **increment** section of the **for** loop normally increments the loop counter variable.

Here is an example of a **for** loop:

```
#include <16C74.h>

void main (void)
{
    int i;
    for(i=0; i<10; i++)
    printf("%d ",i);
    printf ("done");
}
```

This program will print the numbers 0 - 9 on the screen. The program works like this. First the loop counter variable, **i**, is set to zero. Next the expression `i<10` is evaluated. If this statement is true the `printf("%d  ",i);` statement is executed. Each time after the `printf("%d  ",i);` is executed, the loop counter variable is incremented. This whole process continues until the expression `i<10` becomes false. At this point, the for loop is exited and the `printf("done");` statement is executed.

As previously stated, the conditional test is performed at the start of each iteration of the loop. Therefore, if the test is false to start off with, the `for` loop will never be executed.
You are not restricted just to incrementing the counter variable. Here are some variations on the `for` loop:

```
for (num=100; num>0; num=num-1)

for (count=0; count<50; count+=5)

for (count=1; count<=10 && error==false; count++)
```


Converting an example in to assembler to see what happens:

```
int h, a;
for (h=0;h!=10;h++)

    0007:  CLRF    0E     ; clear h
    0008:  MOVLW   0A     ; load 10
    0009:  SUBWF   0E,W   ; subtract from h
    000A:  BTFSC   03,2   ; and test for zero
    000B:  GOTO    00F    ; if i=10, exit loop

a++;
    000C:  INCF    0F,F   ; increment a
    000D:  INCF    0E,F   ; increment h
    000E:  GOTO    008    ; loop again
```

EXCERCISE⇨

1. What do the following `for()` statements do?

```
for(i=1; ;i++)

for(;;)

for(num=1; num; num++)
```

2. Write a program that displays all the factors of a number.

5.5 while Loop

Another of the loops in C is the `while` loop. While an expression is true, the `while` loop repeats a statement or block of code. Hence the name `while`. Here is the general format:

```
while (expression)
    statement;
```

OR

```
while (expression)
    {
    statement;
    }
```

The `expression` is any valid C expression. The value of `expression` is checked prior to each iteration of the statement or block of code. This means that if `expression` is false the statement or block of code does not get executed. Here is an example of a `while` loop.

```
#include <16C74.h>
#use RS232 (Baud=9600, xmit=pin_c6, RCV=pin_c7

void main (void)
{
    char ch;
    printf("Give me a q\n");
    ch=getche();
    while(ch!='q')
        ch=getche();
    printf("Got a q!\n");
}
```

You will notice that the first statement gets a character from the keyboard. Then the expression is evaluated. As long as the value of `ch` is not a `q`, the program will continue to get another character from the keyboard. Once a `q` is received, the `printf()` is executed and the program ends.

EXCERCISE

1. What do the following `while` statements do?

```
a.  while(i<10)
    {
        printf("%d ",i);
        i++;
    }

b.  while(1)
        printf("%d ",i++);
```

2. Write a program that gets characters from the keyboard using the statement `ch=getch();` and prints them to the screen. When a carriage return is encountered, exit the program.

5.6 do-while Loop

The final loop in C is the `do` loop. Here we combine the `do` and `while` as such:

```
do
{
    statements
}
    while (expression)
```

In this case the statements are always executed before `expression` is evaluated. The `expression` may be any valid C expression.

An example of a `do-while` loop is shown:

```
#include <16C74.h>
#use RS232 (Baud=9600, xmit=pin_c6, RCV=pin_c7
```

```
void main(void)
    {
        char ch;
        do
        {
            ch = getche();
        }
            while(ch !='q');
        printf("Got a q!\n");
    }
```

This program is equivalent to the example we gave in Section **5.5.**

EXCERCISE

1. Rewrite both a and b of Exercise 1 in Section 5.5 using a `do-while` loop.

2. Rewrite Exercise 2 in Section 5.5 using a `do-while` loop.

5.7 Nesting Program Control Statements

When the body of a loop contains another loop, the second loop is said to be nested inside the first loop. Any of C's loops or other control statements can be nested inside each other. The ANSI C standard specifies that compilers must have at least 15 levels of nesting. However, most compilers have virtually unlimited levels of nesting.

An example of a nested `for` loop is shown here:

```
i = 0;
while(i < 10)
{
    for(j=0;j<10;j++)
        printf ("%d ",i*10+j);
    i++;
}
```

This routine will print the numbers 00 - 99 on the screen.

EXCERCISE

1. Write a program that gets a character from the keyboard (`ch=getch();`). Each time a character is read, use the ASCII value to print an equal number of periods to the screen. For example, if the letter 'D' is entered (ASCII value of 68), your program would print 68 periods to the screen. When a 'Q' is entered the program completes.

5.8 break Statement

The **break** statement allows you to exit any loop from any point within the body. The **break** statement bypasses normal termination from an expression. When a **break** statement is encountered in a loop, the program jumps to the next statement after the loop.

For example


```
#include <16C74.h>

void main(void)
{
    int i;

    for(i=0;i<50;i++)
    {
        printf("%d ",i);
        if (i==15)
            break;
    }
}
```

this program will print the numbers 0 - 15 on the screen. The **break** statement works with all C loops.

EXCERCISE

1. What does this loop do?

```
for(i=0;1;i++)
```

```
{
    printf("Microchip is great!");
    if(getch() == 'q')
        break;
}
```

2. Write three programs, each using one of C's loops, that count forever but exit when a key is hit. You can use the function `kbhit()` to detect when a key is pressed. `kbhit()` returns a 1 when a key is pressed and a 0 otherwise. `kbhit()` requires the header file `conio.h`.

5.9 continue Statement

Let's assume that when a certain condition occurs in your loop, you want to skip to the end of the loop without exiting the loop. C has provided you with the `continue` statement. When the program encounters this statement, it will skip all statements between the `continue` and the test condition of the loop. For example,

5

```
#include <16C74.h>

void main(void)
{
    int i;
    for(i=0;i<100;i++)
    {
    continue;
    printf("%d ",i);
    }

}
```

This loop will never execute the `printf()` statement. Each time the `continue` is reached, the program skips the `printf()` and evaluates the expression `i<100`.

A `continue` will cause the program to go directly to the test condition for while and `do-while` loops. In a `for` loop, a `continue` will cause the increment part of the loop to be executed and then the conditional test is evaluated.

5.10 switch Statement

The **if** statement is good for selecting between a couple of alternatives, but becomes very cumbersome when many alternatives exist. Again C comes through by providing you with a **switch** statement. A **switch** statement is equivalent to multiple **if-else** statements. The general form for a **switch** statement is:

```
switch (variable)
{
case constant1:
    statement(s);
    break;
case constant2:
    statement(s);
    break;
case constantN:
    statement(s);
    break;
default:
    statement(s);
}
```


The variable is successively tested against a list of integer or character constants. When a match is found, the body of statements associated with that constant is executed until a **break** is encountered. If no match is found, the statements associated with **default** are executed. The **default** is optional. An example of a **switch** is:

```
#include <16C74.h>
#use RS232 (Baud=9600, xmit=pin_c6, RCV=pin_c7

main()
{
   char ch;
  for(;;)
  {
   ch = getch();
   if(ch=='x')
  return 0;
   switch (ch)
  {
```

```
        case '0':
          printf("Sunday\n");
          break;
        case '1':
          printf("Monday\n");
          break;
        case '2':
          printf("Tuesday\n");
          break;
        case '3':
          printf("Wednesday\n");
          break;
        case '4':
          printf("Thursday\n");
          break;
        case '5':
          printf("Friday\n");
          break;
        case '6':
          printf("Saturday\n");
          break;
        default:
          printf("Invalid entry\n");
        }
          }
      }
```

This example will read a number between 1 and 7. If the number is outside of this range, the message `Invalid entry` will be printed. Values within the range will be converted into the day of the week.

Another example used to set the number of characters per line on a LCD display is as follows. The DIP switch is read and the characters per line settings read, separated from the other bits and then used to return the appropriate value to the calling routine.

```
byte cpl_sw_get()              // characters per line
    {
        byte cpl;
    cpl = portd & 0b01110000;// mask unwanted bits
        switch (cpl)           // now act on value decoded
            {
```

5

```
                    case 0x00:    cpl = 8;    break;
                    case 0x10:    cpl = 16;   break;
                    case 0x20:    cpl = 20;   break;
                    case 0x30:    cpl = 28;   break;
                    default   :   cpl = 40;   break;
                    }
        return (cpl);   // send back value to calling routine
}
```

The ANSI standard states that a C compiler must support at least 257 `case` statements. No two `case` statements in the same `switch` can have the same values. Also switch switches can be nested as long as the inner and outer `switches` do not have any conflicts with values. An ANSI compiler must provide at least 15 levels of nesting for switch statements. Here is an example of nested `switches`.

```
switch (a)
{
    case 1:
    switch (b)
    {
        case 0:
            printf("b is false");
            break;
        case 1:
            printf("b is true");
            break;
    }
    break;
    case 2:
    .
    .
    .
```

5

The `break` statement within the `switch` statement is also optional. This means that two `case` statements can share the same portion of code. An example is provided to illustrate this.

```
#include <16C74.h>
##use RS232 (Baud=9600, xmit=pin_c6, RCV=pin_c7
```

```
void main (void)
{
    int a=6,b=3;
    char ch;
    printf(“A = Addition\n”);
    printf(“S = Subtraction\n”);
    printf(“M = Multiplication\n”);
    printf(“D = Division\n”);
    printf(“Enter choice: ”);
    ch=getche();

    switch (ch)
    {
        case ‘S’:
            b=-b;
            break;
        case ‘A’:
            printf (“\t\t%d”,a+b);
            break;
        case ‘M’:
            printf(“\t\t%d”,a*b);
            break;
        case ‘D’:
            printf (“\t\t%d”, a/b);
            break;
        default:
            printf(“\t\tSay what?”);
        }
    }
```


EXCERCISE

1. What is wrong with this segment of code?

```
float f;

switch(f)
{
    case 10.05:
        .
        .
```

2. Use a **switch** statement to print out the value of a coin. The value of the coin is held in the variable **coin.** The phrases to describe coins are: penny, nickel, dime, quarter, dollar.

3. What are the advantages of using a **switch** statement over many **if-else** statements?

5.11 null Statement (;)

The null statement is a statement containing only a semicolon; it may appear wherever a statement is expected. Nothing happens when the null statement is executed - unlike the NOP in assembler which introduces a 1 cycle delay.

Statements such as **do, for, if** and **while** require that an executable statement appears as the statement body. The null statement satisfies the syntax in those cases.


```
for (i=0;i<10;line[++]=0)
    ;
```

In this example, the loop expression of the **for line[++]=0** initalises the first 10 elements of line to 0. The statement body is a null since no additional commands are required.

5.12 return Statement

The **return** statement terminates the execution of a function and returns control to the calling routine. A value can be returned to the calling function if required but if one is omitted, the returned value is then undefined. If no return is included in the called function, control is still passed back to the calling function after execution of the last line of code. If a returned value is not required, declare the function to have a **void** return type.

```
GetValue(c)
    int c;
    {
    c++;
```

```
        return c;
        }

    void GetNothing(c)
    int c;
        {
        c++;
        return;
        }

main()
    {
        int x;
        x = GetValue();
        GetNothing();
    }
```

NOTES

Arrays and Strings

In this chapter you will learn about arrays. An array is simply a list of related variables of the same data type. Since strings are arrays of characters with some special rules, we will discuss them now.

Topics that will be discussed:

Arrays
Strings
One-dimensional Arrays
Multidimensional Arrays
Initialization

6

6.1 One-Dimensional Arrays

An array is a list of variables that are all of the same type and can be referenced through the same name. An individual variable in the array is called an array element. This is a simple way to handle groups of related data.

The general form for declaring one-dimensional arrays is:

```
type var_name [size];
```

where **type** is a valid C data type, **var_name** is the name of the array, and **size** specifies how many elements are in the array. For instance, if we want an array of 50 elements we would use this statement.

```
int height[50];
```

When an array is declared, C defines the first element to be at an index of 0. If the array has 50 elements, the last element is at an index of 49. Using the above example, say I want to index the 25th element of the array **height** and assign a value of 60. The following example shows how to do this.

6

```
height [24] = 60;
```

C stores one-dimensional arrays in contiguous memory locations. The first element is at the lowest address. If the following segment of code is executed

```
int num[10];
int i;
for(i=0;i<10;i++)

    0007:  CLRF    18     ; clear i
    0008:  MOVLW   0A
    0009:  SUBWF   18,W   ; now test if = 10
    000A:  BTFSC   03,0
    000B:  GOTO    013    ; if so then stop routine
```

```
num[i] = i ;

    000C:   MOVLW   0E    ; load start of num area
    000D:   ADDWF   18,W
    000E:   MOVWF   04
    000F:   MOVF    18,W
    0010:   MOVWF   00
    0011:   INCF    18,F
    0012:   GOTO    008
```

array `i` will look like this in memory.

```
element 1  2  3  4  5  6  7  8  9  10
        0  1  2  3  4  5  6  7  8  9
```

Any array element can be used anywhere you would use a variable or constant. Here is another example program. It simply assigns the square of the index to the array element, then prints out all elements.

```
#include <16C74.h>

void main(void)
{
    int num[10];
    int i;

    for(i=0;i<10;i++)
        num[i] = i * i;

    for(i=0;i<10;i++)
        printf("%d ",num[i]);
}
```

What happens if you have an array with ten elements and you accidently write to the eleventh element? C has no bounds checking for array indexes. Therefore you may read or write to an element not declared in the array, however this will generally have disastrous results. Often this will cause the program to crash and sometimes even the computer.

C does not allow you to assign the value of one array to another simply by using an assignment like:

```
int a[10],b[10];
.
.
a=b;
```

The above example is wrong. If you want to copy the contents of one array into another, you must copy each individual element from the first array into the second array. The following example shows how to copy the array `a[ ]` into `b[ ]` assuming that each array has 20 elements.

```
for(i=0;i<20;i++)
    b[i] = a[i];
```

EXCERCISE

1. What is wrong with the following segment of code?

```
int i;

char count[10];

for(i=0;i<100;i++)
    count[i] = getch();
```


2. Write a program that first reads 10 characters from the keyboard using `getch()`. The program will report if any of these characters match.

6.2 Strings

The most common one-dimensional array is the string. C does not have a built in string data type. Instead, it supports strings using one-dimensional arrays of characters. A string is defined as a null terminated character array. A null in C is defined as a 0. If every string must be terminated by a null, then when that string is declared you must add an extra element. This extra element will hold the null. All string constants are automatically null terminated by the C compiler.

Since we are using strings, how can you input a string into your program using the keyboard? The function `gets(str)` will read characters from the keyboard until a carriage return is encountered. The string of characters that was read will be stored in the declared array `str`. You must make sure that the length of `str` is greater than or equal to the number of characters read from the keyboard and the null (`null = \0`).

Let's illustrate how to use the function `gets()` with an example.

```
#include <16C74.h>

void main(void)
{
    char str[80];
    int i;

    printf("Enter a string (<80 chars):\n");
    gets(str);
    for(i=0; str[i] ;i++)
        printf("%c",str[i]);
    printf("\n%s",str);
}
```

Here we see that the string can be printed in two ways: as an array of characters using the `%c` or as a string using the `%s`.

EXCERCISE

1. What is wrong with this program? The function `strcpy()` copies the second argument into the first argument.

```
#include <16C74.h>
#include <string.h>

void main(void)
{
    char str[10];

    strcpy(str, "Motorola who?");
    printf(str);

}
```

2. Write a program that reads a string of characters from the screen and prints them in reverse order on the screen.

6.3 Multidimensional Arrays

C is not limited to one-dimensional arrays. You can create two or more dimensions. For example, to create an integer array called `number` with 5x5 elements, you would use:

```
int number[5][5];    //uses 25 ram locations
```

Additional dimensions can be added simply by attaching another set of brackets.
For simplicity, we will discuss only two-dimensional arrays but everything can be applied to multidimensional arrays. A two-dimensional array is best represented by a row, column format. Therefore, two-dimensional arrays are accessed a row at a time, from left to right. The following figure shows a graphical representation of a 5x5 array.

Two-dimensional arrays are used just like one-dimensional arrays. For example, the following program loads a 5x4 array with the product of the indices, then displays the contents of the array in row, column format.

```
void main(void)
{
    int array[5][4];
    int i,j;

    for(i=0;i<5;i++)
        for(j=0;j<4;j++)
            array[i] [3]=i*j;
        for(i=0;i<5;i++)
        {
            for(j=0;j<4;j++)
                printf("%d ",array[i][j]);
            printf("\n");
        }
}
```

The output of this program should look like this:

```
0   0   0   0
0   1   2   3
0   2   4   6
0   3   6   9
0   4   8   12
```

As you can see, when using the multidimensional arrays the number of variables needed to access each individual element increases. Due to the PIC's memory map, arrays of 100 or 10x10 are not possible, however, two 50 arrays would fit.

EXCERCISE

1. Write a program that declares a 3x3x3 array and loads it with the numbers 1 to 27. Print the array to the screen.

2. Using the program from Exercise 1, print out the sum of each row and column.

6.4 Initializing Arrays

So far you have seen only individual array elements having values assigned. C provides a method in which you can assign an initial value to an array just like you would for a variable. The general form for one-dimensional arrays is shown here:

```
type array_name[size] = (value_list);
```

The `value_list` is a comma separated list of constants that are compatible with the type of the array. The first constant will be placed in the first element, the second constant in the second element and so on. The following example shows a 5 element integer array initialization.

```
int i[5] = (1,2,3,4,5);
```

The element `i[0]` will have a value of 1 and the element `i[4]` will have a value of 5.

A string (character array) can be initialized in two ways. First you may make a list of each individual character as such:

```
char str[3] (‘a’, ‘b’, ‘c’);
```

The second method is to use a quoted string, as shown here

```
char name [5] = “John”;
```

You may have noticed that no curly braces enclosed the string. They are not used in this type of initialization because strings in C must end with a null. The compiler automatically appends a null at the end of `“John”`.

Multidimensional arrays are initialized in the same way as one-dimensional arrays. It is probably easier to simulate a row, column format when using two-dimensional arrays. The following example shows a 3x3 array initialisation.

```
int num[3] [3]=( 1, 2, 3,
                 4, 5, 6,
                 7, 8, 9);
```

EXCERCISE

1. Is this declaration correct?

```
int count[3] = 10.0, 5.6, 15.7;
```

2. Write a program that has a lookup table for the square and the cube of a number. Each row should have the number, the square of the number and the cube of the number. Create a 9x3 array to hold the information for numbers 1-9. Ask the user for a number using the statement `scanf(“%d”, &num);`. Then print out the number and its square and cube.

6.5 Arrays of Strings

Arrays of strings are very common in C. They can be declared and initialized like any other array. The way in which you use the array is somewhat different from other arrays. For instance, what does the following declaration define?

```
char names [10] [40];
```

This statement specifies that the array `name` 5 contains 10 names up to 40 characters long (including the null). To access a string from this table, specify only the first index. For example, to print the fifth name from this array, use the following statement.

```
printf ("%s",names[4]);
```

The same follows for arrays with greater than two dimensions. For instance, if the array `animals` was declared as such:

```
char animals[5][4][80];
```

To access a specific string, you would use the first two dimensions. For example, to access the second string in the third list, specify `animals[2][1]`.

EXCERCISE

1. Write a program that creates a string table containing the words for the numbers 0 through 9. Allow the user to enter a single digit number and then your program will display the respective word. To obtain an index into the table, subtract '0' from the character entered.

6.6 string functions

Strings can be manipulated in a number of ways within a program. One example is copying from a source to a destination via the `strcpy` command. This allows a constant string to be inputted into RAM.

```
#include  <string.h> // the library for string
                     // functions
char string[10];     // define string array
.
.
strcpy (string, "Hi There");// set up characters into string
```

Note that pointers to ROM are not valid in the PIC so you can not pass a constant string to one of these functions. **STRLEN("HI")** is not valid. More examples:

```
char s1[10], s2[10];

strcpy(s1, "abc");
strcpy(s2, "def");
strcat(s1,s2);
printf("%u",strlen(s1));      // will print 6
printf(s1);                   // will print abcdef

if(strcmp(s1,s2)!=0)
    printf("no match"); will print
```

Some other string functions are available such as :-

strcat Appends two strings
strchr Looks for first occurance of a character
strrchr Finds last occurance of a character
strcmp Compare two strings
strncmp Compare a number of characters in two strings
stricmp Compares two strings ignoring their case (UPPER vs lower)
strncpy Copies a number of characters from one string to another
strlen Calculates the length of a string
strlwr Replaces upper case with lower case letters
strpbrk Locate the first matching character in two strings
strstr Locate the first occurance of a character sequence in a string

Ensure the string arrays match the size of the strings being manipulated.

Pointers

This chapter covers one of the most important and most troublesome feature of C, the pointer. A pointer is basically the address of some object.

Some of the topics we will cover in this chapter are:

Pointer basics
Pointers and arrays
Passing pointers to functions

7

7.1 Introduction to Pointers

A pointer is a memory location (variable) that holds the address of another memory location. For example, if a pointer variable called `a` contains the address of a variable called `b`, then `a` points to `b`. If `b` is a variable at location 100 in memory, then `a` would contain the value 100.

The general form to declare a pointer variable is:

```
type *var_name;
```

The `type` of a pointer is one of the valid C data types. It specifies the type of variables to which `var_name` can point. You may have noticed that `var_name` is preceded by an `*`. This tells the compiler that `var_name` is a pointer variable. For example, the following statement creates a pointer to an integer.

```
int *ptr;
```

The two special operators that are associated with pointers are the `*` and the `&`. The address of a variable can be accessed by preceding the variable with the `&` operator. The `*` operator returns the value stored at the address pointed to by the variable. For example,

```
#include <16C74.h>

void main(void)
{
    int *a,b;     //more than 1 byte may be assigned to a
    b = 6;
    a = &b;
    printf("%d",*a);
}
```


NOTE

By default, the compiler uses one byte for pointers. This means only locations 0-255 can be pointed to. For parts with larger memory a two-byte (16-bit) pointer may need to be used. To select 16 bit pointers, use the following directive:

```
#device   *=16
```

Be aware more ROM code will be generated since 16 bit arithmetic is less efficient.

The first statement declares two variables: `a`, which is an integer pointer and `b`, which is an integer. The next statement assigns the value of 6 to `b`. Then the address of `b (&b)` is assigned to the pointer variable `a`. This line can be read as assign `a` the address of `b`. Finally, the value of `b` is displayed to the screen by using the `*` operator with the pointer variable `a`. This line can print the value at the address pointed to by `a`. This process of referencing a value through a pointer is called indirection. A graphical example is shown here.

100	**3**	**i**
102	**5**	**j**
104	**-1**	**k**
106	**102**	**ptr**

```
    int i, j, k;
    int *ptr;
```
Initially
```
    i is 3
    &i is 100         // the location of i
```

As `ptr` contains `102`
```
    ptr is 102        // the value pointed to by the
                      // location in ptr
    *ptr is 5
```

It is also possible to assign a value to a memory location by using a pointer. For instance, let's restructure the previous program in the following manner:

```
#include <16C74.h>

void main (void)
{
    int *a,b;
    a = &b;
    *a = 6;
    printf("%d",b);
}
```

In this program, we first assign the address of variable `b` to `a`, then we assign a value to b by using `a`. The line `*a = 6;` can be read as assign the value 6 to the memory location pointed to by `a`. Obviously, the use of a pointer in the previous two examples is not necessary but it illustrates the usage of pointers.

EXCERCISE

1. Write a program with a `for` loop that counts from 0 to 9 and displays the numbers on the screen. Print the numbers using a pointer.

7.2 Restrictions to Pointers

In general, pointers may be treated like other variables. However, there are a few rules and exceptions that you must understand. In addition to the `*` and `&` operators, there are only four other operators that can be applied to pointer variables: `+, ++, -, - -`. Only integer quantities may be added or subtracted from pointer variables.

When a pointer variable is incremented, it points to the next memory location. If we assume that the pointer variable `p` contains the address 100, after the statement

```
p++;
```

executes, `p` will have a value of 102 assuming that integers are two bytes long. If `p` had been a `float` pointer, `p` would contain the value 104 after the increment assuming that floating point numbers are four bytes long. The only pointer arithmetic that appears as expected is for the `char` type, because characters are only one byte long.

You can add or subtract any integer value you wish, to or from a pointer. For example, the following statement

```
int *p;
.
.
p = p+200;
```

causes **p** to point to the 200th memory location past the one to which **p** was previously pointing.

It is possible to increment or decrement either the pointer itself or the object to which it points. You must be careful when incrementing or decrementing the object pointed to by a pointer. What do you think the following statement will do if the value of **ptr** is **1** before the statement is executed?

```
*p++;
```

This statement first increments **p** and then gets the value pointed to at the new location. To increment the object that is pointed to by a pointer, use the following statement:

```
(*p)++;
```

The parenthesis cause the value that is pointed to by **p** to be incremented. This is due to the precedence of ***** versus **++**.

Pointers may also be used in relational operations. However, they only make sense if the pointers relate to each other, i.e. they both point to the same object.

Pointers can not be created to ROM. For example, the following is illegal:

```
char  CONST  name[S] = "JOHN";
      ....
ptr=&name[0];
```

This is valid without the **CONST**. The **CONST** puts the data into ROM.

EXCERCISE

1. Declare the following variables and assign the address of the variable to the pointer variable. Print the value of each pointer variable using the **%p**. Then increment each pointer and print out the value of the

pointer variable again. What are the sizes of each of the data types on your machine?

```
char *cp,ch;
int *ip,i;
float *fp,f;
double *dp,d;
```

2. What is wrong with this fragment?

```
int *p,i;

p = &i;

p = p/2;
```

7.3 Pointers and Arrays

In C, pointers and arrays are closely related and are sometimes interchangeable. It is this relationship between the two that makes the power of C even more apparent.

If you use an array name without an index, you are actually using a pointer to the beginning of the array. In the last chapter, we used the function `gets()`, in which we passed only the name of the string. What is actually passed to the function is a pointer to the first element in the string. This is a very important note: when an array is passed to a function, only a pointer to the first element is passed. They can't be created for use with constant arrays or structures.

Since an array name without an index is a pointer, you can assign that value to another pointer. This would allow you to access the array using pointer arithmetic. For instance,

```
#include <16C74.h>

int a[5]={1,2,3,4,5};

void main(void)
```

```
{
    int *p,i;
    p = a;
    for(i=0;i<5;i++)
        printf ("%d",*(p+i));
}
```

This is a perfectly valid C program. You will notice that in the `printf()` statement we use `* (p+i)`, where `i` is the index of the array. You may be surprised that you can also index a pointer as if it were an array. The following program is valid.

```
#include <16C74.h>

int a[5]={1,2,3,4,5};
void main (void)
{
    int *p,i;
    p = a;
    for(i=0;i<5;i++)
        printf("%d",p[i]);
}
```

One thing to remember is that a pointer should only be indexed when it points to an array. Since pointers to arrays point only to the first element or base of the string, it is invalid to increment the pointer. Therefore, this statement would be invalid for the previous program.

```
p++;
```

Mixing pointers and arrays will produce unpredictable results. The following examples show the problem - the second version does not mix pointers and arrays:

```
int *p;
int array[8];
p = array;
    0007:  MOVLW   0F    ; load start of array
    0008:  MOVWF   0E    ; pointer
*p = 3;
    0009:  MOVF    0E,W  ;
```

```
    000A:  MOVWF  04    ; point at indirect reg
    000B:  MOVLW  03    ; load 3
    000C:  MOVWF  00    ; and save at pointed location
array[1] = 4;
    000D:  MOVLW  04    ; load 4
    000E:  MOVWF  10    ; into first location of array

int *p;
int array[8];
p = array;
    0007:  MOVLW  0F
    0008:  MOVWF  0E
p[1] = 3;
    0009:  MOVLW  01    ; load array position
    000A:  ADDWF  0E,W  ; add to array start position
    000B:  MOVWF  04    ; load into array pointer
    000C:  MOVLW  03    ; load in 3
    000D:  MOVWF  00    ; save in location pointed to
                          *(array+1) = 4;
    000E:  MOVLW  10    ; load array position
    000F:  MOVWF  04    ; point to it
    0010:  MOVLW  04    ; load 4
    0011:  MOVWF  00    ; save in pointed to location
```

EXCERCISE⇨

1. Is this segment of code correct?

```
int count[10];
.
.
count = count+2;
```


2. What value does this segment of code display?

```
int value[5]=(5,10,15,20,25);
int *p;

p = value;
printf("%d",*p+3);
```

7.4 Passing Pointers to Functions

In Section 3, we talked about the two ways that arguments can be passed to functions, "call by value" and "call by reference". The second method passes the address to the function, or in other words a pointer is passed to the function. At this point any changes made to the variable using the pointer actually change the value of the variable from the calling routine. Pointers may be passed to functions just like any other variables. The following example shows how to pass a string to a function using pointers.

```
#include <16C74.h>

void puts(char *p);

void main(void)
{
    puts("Microchip is great!");
}

void puts(char *p)
{
    while(*p)
    {
        printf("%c", *p);
        p++;
    }
    printf("\n");
}
```

In this example, the pointer `p` points to the first character in the string, the "`M`". The statement `while(*p)` is checking for the null at the end of the string. Each time through the while loop, the character that is pointed to by `p` is printed. Then `p` is incremented to point to the next character in the string.

Another example of passing a pointer to a function is:

```
void IncBy10(int *n)
{
    *n += 10;
```

```
}

void main(void)
{
    int i=0;
    IncBy10(i);
}
```

The above example may be rewritten to enhance readability using a special kind of pointer parameter called a reference parameter. Example:

```
void incby10(int & n)
{
    n+=10;
}

void main(void)
{
    int i=0;

    incby10(i);
}
```

Both of the above examples show how to return a value from a function via the parameter list.

EXCERCISE⇨

1. Write a program that passes a `float` value to a function. Inside the function, the value of -1 is assigned to the function parameter. After the function returns to `main`, print the value of the `float` variable.

2. Write a program that passes a `float` pointer to a function. Inside the function, the value of -1 is assigned to the variable. After the function returns to `main()`, print the value of the `float` variable.

Structures and Unions

Structures and unions represent two of C's most important user defined types. Structures are a group of related variables that can have different data types. Unions are a group of variables that share the same memory space.

In this chapter we will cover:

Structure basics
Pointers to Structures
Nested Structures
Union basics
Pointers to Unions

8.1 Introduction to Structures

A structure is a group of related items that can be accessed through a common name. Each of the items within a structure has its own data types, which can be different from each other. C defines structures in the following way:

```
struct tag-name
{
    type element1;
    type element2;
    .
    .
    type elementn;
}   variable-list;
```

The keyword **struct** tells the compiler that a structure is about to be defined. Within the structure each **type** is one of the valid data types. These types do not need to be the same. The **tag-name** is the name of the structure. The **variable-list** declares some variables that have a data type of **struct tag-name**. The **variable-list** is optional. Each of the items in the structure is commonly referred to as fields or members. We will refer to them as members.

In general the information stored in a structure is logically related. For example, you might use a structure to hold the name, address and telephone number of all your customers. The following example is for a card catalog in a library.

```
struct catalog
{
    char author[40];
    char title[40];
    char pub[40];
    unsigned int date;
    unsigned char rev;
} card;
```

In this example the name of the structure is **catalog**. It is not the name of a variable, only the name of this type of structure.

The variable **card** is declared as a structure of type **catalog**.

To access any member of a structure, you must specify both the name of the variable and the name of the member. These names are separated by a period. For example, to access the revision member of the structure **catalog**, you would use:

```
card.rev='a';
```

where **card** is the variable name and rev is the member. The operator is used to access members of a structure. To print the author member of the structure catalog, you would type:

```
printf ("Author is %s\n",card.author);
```

Now that we know how to define, declare and access a structure, what does a structure look like in memory? The following shows what the structure **catalog** looks like in memory.

author	40 bytes
title	40 bytes
pub	40 bytes
date	2 bytes
rev	1 byte

If you wanted to get the address of the date member of the **card** structure you would use **&card.date**. If you want to print the name of the publisher, you would use **printf("%s",card.pub).** What if you wanted to access a specific element in the title, like the 3rd. element in the string?

```
card.title[2];
```

The first element of title is 0, the second is 1 and, finally, the third is 2.

Once you have defined a structure, you can create more structure variables anywhere in the program using:

```
struct tag-name var-list;
```

For instance, if the structure catalog was defined earlier in the program, you can define two more variables like this:

```
struct catalog book,list;
```

C allows you to declare arrays of structures just like any other data type. This example declares a 50-element array of the structure **catalog**.

```
struct catalog big[50];
```

If you wanted to access an individual structure within the array, you would index the structure variable, i.e. **big[10].** How would you access the title member of the 10th element of the structure array big?

```
big[9].title
```

Structures may also be passed to functions. A function can return a structure just like any other data type. You can also assign the values of one structure to another simply by using an assignment. The following fragment is perfectly valid.

```
struct temp
{
    int a;
    float b;
    char c;
}   var1,var2;

vari.a = 37;
var2.b = 53.65;

var2 = var1;
```

8

After this fragment of code executes the structure, variable **var2** will have the same contents as **var1**.

This is an example of initializing a structure.

```
struct example
{
    char who[50];
```

```
        char ch;
        int i;
    } var1[2]={"Rodger",'Y',27,"Jack",'N',30};
```

One important thing to note is that when you pass a structure to a function, the entire structure is passed by the "call by value" method. Therefore, any modification of the structure in the function will not affect the value of the structure in the calling routine. The number of elements in a structure does not affect the way it is passed to a function.

An example of using this on the PIC to set up an LCD interface would be

```
struct cont_pins
{
boolean en1;           // enable for all displays
boolean en2;           // enable for 40x4 line displays
boolean rs;            // register select
int data:4;
} cont;

#byte cont = 8         // Control on port d
```

This sets the structure for **cont_pins** and is then handled within the program

NOTE

The **:4** notation for data indicates **4 bits** are to be allocated for that item. In this case **D0** will be **en1**, and **D3-6** will be **data**.

```
void LcdSendNibble(byte n)
   {
   cont.data = n;          // present data
   delay_cycles(1);        // delay
   cont.en1 = 1;           // set en1 line high
   delay_us(2);            // delay
   cont.en1 = 0;           // set en1 line low
   }
```

EXCERCISE⇨

1. Write a program that has a structure with one character and a string of 40 characters. Read a character from the keyboard and save it in the character using `getch()`. Read a string and save it in the string using `gets()`. Then print the values of the members.

2. What is wrong with this section of code?

```
struct type
{
    int i;
    long l;
    char str[50];
}   s;
    .
    .
    .
i=10;
```

8.2 Pointers to Structures

Sometimes it is very useful to access a structure through a pointer. Pointers to structures are declared in the same way that pointers to other data types are declared. For example, the following section of code declares a structure variable **p** and a structure pointer variable **q** with structure type of **temp**.

```
struct temp
{
    int i;
    char ch;
} p,*q;
```

Using this definition of the temp structure, the statement **q=&p** is perfectly valid. Now that **q** points to **p**, you can access **p** through **q**. If you want to access an individual member of **p**, you must use the arrow operator as shown here.

```
q->i=1;
```

This statement would assign a value of 1 to the member `i` of the variable `p`. Notice that the arrow operator is a minus sign followed by a greater-than sign without any spaces in between.

Since C passes the entire structure to a function, large structures can reduce the program execution speed because of the relatively large data transfer. For this reason, it is easier to pass a pointer to the structure to the function.
One important thing to note is: When accessing a structure member using a structure variable, use the period. When accessing a structure member using a pointer to the structure, you must use the arrow operator.

This example shows how a pointer to a structure is utilized.

```
#include <16C74.h>
#include <string.h>

struct s_type
{
    int i;
    char str[80];
} s,*p;

void main (void)
{
    p=&s;
    s.i=10;
    p->i=10;

    strcpy(p->str,”I like structures”);
    printf(“%d %d %s”,s.i,p->i,p->str);
}
```

The two lines `s.i=10` and `p->i=10` are equivalent.

EXCERCISE⇨

1. Is this segment of code correct?

```
struct S_type
{
```

```
        int a;
        int b;
} s,*p;

void main(void)
{
        p=&s;
        p.a=100;
}
```

2. Write a program that creates an array of structures three long of the type PIC. You will need to load the structures with a PICl6C5X, PICl6CXX, and a PICl7CXX device. The user will select which structure to print using the keyboard to input a 1, 2, or 3. The format of the structure is:

```
struct PIC
  {
  char name[20];
  unsigned char progmem;
  unsigned char datamem;
  char feature[80];
  };
```

8.3 Nesting Structures

So far, you have only seen that members of a structure were one of the C data types. However, the members of structures can also be other structures. This is called nesting structures. For example,

```
#define NUM_OF_PICS 25

struct PIC
{
        char name[40];
        unsigned char progmem;
        unsigned char datamem;
        char feature[80];
};

struct products
{
        struct PlC devices[NUM_OF_PICS];
```

```
        char package_type[40];
        float cost;
    } list1;
```

The structure products has three elements: an array of `PIC` structures called `devices`, a string that has the package name and the cost. These elements can be accessed using the `list1` variable.

8.4 Introduction to Unions

A union is defined as a single memory location that is shared by two or more variables. The variables that share the memory location may be of different data types. However, you may only use one variable at a time. A union looks very much like a structure. The general format of the union is:

```
    union tag-name
    {
        type element1;
        type element2;
             .
             .
        type elementn;
    } variable-list;
```

Again, the `tag-name` is the name of the union and the `variable-list` are the variables that have a union type `tag-name`. The difference between unions and structures is that each member of the union shares the same data space. For example, the following union contains three members: an integer, a character array and a double.

```
    union u_type
    {
        int i;
        char c[3];
        double d;
    } temp;
```

The way that a union appears in memory is shown below. We will use the previous example to illustrate a union. The integer uses two bytes, the character array uses three bytes and the double uses four bytes.

d			
c[2]	c[1]	c[0]	
i			
element 0	element 1	element 2	element 3

Accessing the members of the union is the same as with structures, you use a period. The statement **`temp.i`** will access the two byte integer member **`i`** of the union **`temp`** and **`temp.d`** will access the four byte double **`d`**. If you are accessing the union through a pointer, you would use the arrow operator just like structures.

It is important to note that the size of the union is fixed at compile time to accommodate the largest member of the union. Assuming that doubles are four bytes long, the union **`temp`** will have a length of four bytes.

A good example of using a union is when an 8-bit microcontroller has an external 12-bit A/D converter connected to a serial port. The microcontroller reads the A/D in two bytes. So we might set up a union that has two **`unsigned chars`** and a **`signed short`** as the members.

```
union sample
{
     unsigned char bytes[2];
     signed short word;
}
```

When you want to read the A/D, you would read two bytes of data from the A/D and store them in the **`bytes`** array. Then, whenever you want to use the 12-bit sample you would use **`word`** to access the 12-bit number.

EXCERCISE

1. What are the differences between a structure and an union? What is the same?

2. Write a program that has a union with a **`long int`** member and an four byte character array. Your program should print the **`long int`** to the screen a byte at a time.

PIC Specific C

Having understood the basics of C, it is now time to move into the PIC specific settings, functions and operations. Every compiler has its own good and not so good points.

The CCS version has an extensive range of inbuilt functions to save time and speed up the learning process for newcomers and part time C programmers.

In this chapter we will cover:

Inputs and Outputs
Mixing C and Assembler
A/D Conversion
Data Communications
PWM
LCD Driving
Interrupts
Include Libraries

9.1 Inputs and Outputs

The Input and Output ports on a PIC are made up from two registers - PORT and PORT DIRECTION - and are designated PORTA,B,C,D,E and TRISA,B,C,D,E. Their availability depends upon the PIC being used in the design. An 8 pin PIC has a single GPIO register and TRIS register - 6 I/O lines. The 16C74 has PORTS A,B,C,D and E - 33 I/O lines. A block diagram of PORTA is shown below. Ports B,C,D and E are similar but the data sheet needs to be consulted for PIC specifics.

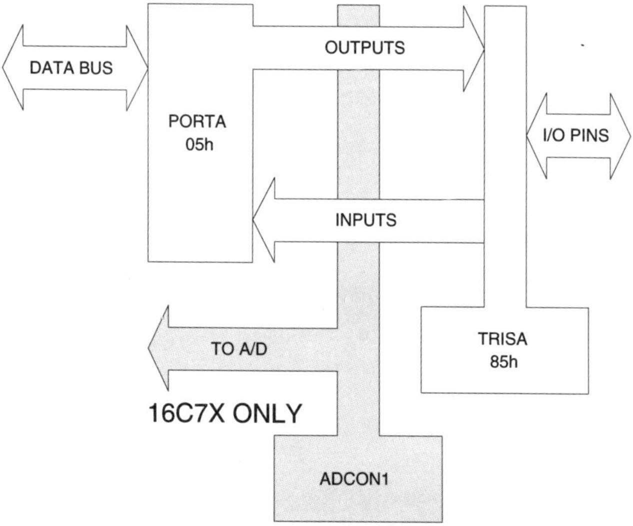

Port A has a 5 or 6 lines - depending on the PIC - which can be configured as either inputs or outputs. Configuration of the port direction is via the TRISA register. Inputs are set with a 1 and outputs are set with a 0. The pins have both source and sink capability of typically 25mA per pin.

The exception to the I/O lines is the A4 pin which has an open collector output. As a result, the voltage levels on the pin - if tied high with a resistor - is inverted to the bit in the PORTA register. i.e. a logic 1 in porta,4 turns on the transistor and hence pulls the pin low.

An example in assembler could be

```
clrfporta                   ; set outputs low
page1                       ; select register page 1
movlw     b'00000011'       ; A0,1 as inputs, A2-4 as outputs
movwf     porta             ; send w to port control register
page0                       ; change back to register page 0
```

Data is sent to the port via a `movwf porta` and bits can be individually manipulated with either `bsf` or `bcf`. Data is read from the port with either `movfw porta` or bit testing with `btfss` or `btfsc`.

NOTE On devices with A/D converters, ensure ADCON1 register is also set correctly an the I/O default is ANALOG.

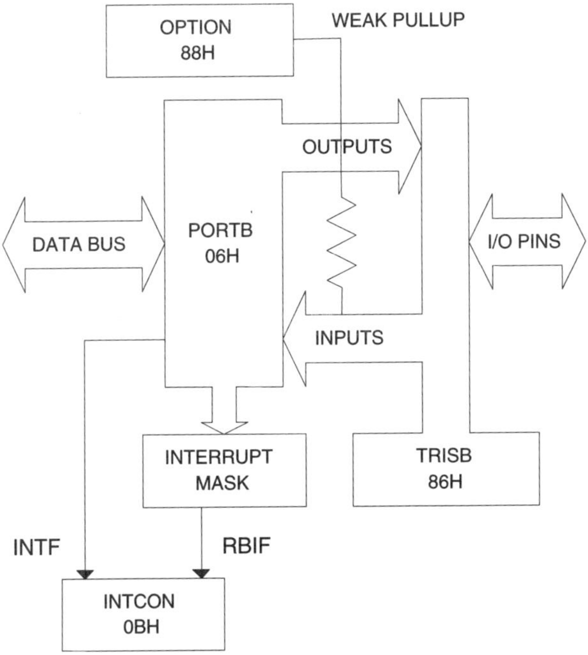

Port B block diagram

Port C is similar but does not have the pull-up and interrupt capability of Port B. It does have the additional PIC hardware functions as alternatives to being used as an 8 bit port.

9

Other uses for Port C I/O pins

C0	C1	C2	C3	C4	C5	C6	C7
I/O	I/O	I/O	I/O	I/O	I/O	I/O	I/O
T1OSO	T1OSI	CCP1	SCK	SDI	SDO	TX	RX
T1CKI	CCP2	PWM1	SCL	SDA		CK	DT
	PWM2						

The C compiler can interpret inputs and outputs in a number of ways - fixed, fast or standard. In standard mode, the port direction registers are set up prior to each I/O operation. This adds lines to a program and hence slows down the speed, but improves the safety side of the code by ensuring the I/O lines are always set as specified.

Fast I/O enables the user to set the port direction and this remains in place until re- defined. The compiler does not add lines of code to setup the port direction prior to each I/O operation.

The following example sets PORTB as inputs and then reads in the value.

```
set_tris_b(0xff);              // make inputs
b_rate = portb ;               // read in port
```

Bit masking is easily achieved by adding the `&` and the pattern to mask after the port name

```
b_rate = portb & 0b00000011;   // mask out unwanted bits
```

The value stored in `b_rate` can then be used to set up a value to return to the calling function. The following is the whole function used to read some dip switches and set up a baud rate for a comms routine.

```
byte bd_sw_get()               // baud rate selection
    {
    byte b_rate;
    b_rate = portb & 0b00000011;// mask out unwanted bits
    switch(b_rate)
```

```
        {
        case 0: set_uart_speed(1200);
            break;
        case 1: set_uart_speed(2400);
            break;
        case 2: set_uart_speed(4800);
            break;
        case 3: set_uart_speed(9600);
            break;
        }
    }
```

When setting up ports, it is advisable to set up the port conditions before the port direction registers (TRIS). This prevents the port outputting an unwanted condition prior to being set. When setting bit patterns in registers or ports, work in binary as this will make it easier for you writing and others reading the source code. It also saves converting between number bases.

Manipulation of data to and from the I/O ports is made easy with the use of numerous built in functions. On a bit level there are: -

`bit_set(variable, bit) ;`	used to set a bit
`bit_clear(variable, bit) ;`	used to clear a bit
`bit_test(variable, bit) ;`	used to test a bit

The above three can be used on variables and I/O

`b = input(pin ;`	get the state or value of a pin
`output_bit(pin, value) ;`	set a port pin to a specific value
`output_float(pin) ;`	set a pin to input or floating mode
`output_high(pin) ;`	set an output to logic 1
`output_low(pin) ;`	set an output to logic 0

On a port wide basis, the following instructions are used:-

`port_b_pullups(true/false) ;`	enables or disables the weak pullup on port b
`set_tris_a(value) ;`	sets the combination of inputs and outputs for a given port – set a 1

for input and 0 for output. This applies to ports b – g.

Port direction registers are configured every time a port is accessed unless the following pre-processor directives are used:-

#use fast_io(port) leaves the state of the port the same unless re-configured

#use fixed_io(port_outputs=pin, pin) perminantly sets up the data direction register for the port

#use standard_io(port) default for configuring the port every time it's used

9.2 Mixing C and Assembler

There are times when inline assembler code is required in the middle of a C program. The reasons could be for code compactness, timing constraints or simply because a routine works 'as is'. The following example finds the parity of a value **d** passed to the routine **FindParity** which is then equated to **a** when the routine is called.

```
    FindParity(byte d)
    {
    byte  count;
    #asm
        movlw       8
        movwf       count
        clrw
    loop:
        xorwf       d,w
        rrf         d,f
        decfsz      count,f
        goto        loop
        movwf       _return_
    #endasm
    }
main()
{
byte a, d=7;
```

```
    a = FindParity(d);

}
```

When compiled, the program looks like:-

```
    FindParity(byte d)
        {
            byte  count;
            #asm
                        0005:  MOVLW   08
                        0006:  MOVWF   28
                        0007:  CLRW
                        0008:  XORWF   27,W
                        0009:  RRF     27,F
                        000A:  DECFSZ  28,F
                        000B:  GOTO    008
            #endasm
                        000C:  MOVWF   21
                        000E:  GOTO    016
        }
    main()
        {
                        0011:  MOVLW   07
                        0012:  MOVWF   26
    byte a, d=7;
    a = FindParity(d);
                        0013:  MOVF    26,W
                        0014:  MOVWF   27
                        0015:  GOTO    005
                        0016:  MOVF    21,W
                        0017:  MOVWF   25
        }
```

Key to PIC16Cxx Family Instruction Sets

Field	Description	
b	Bit address within an 8 bit file register (0-7)	
d	Destination select;	d = 0 Store result in W
		d = 1 Store result in file register f (default)
		Assembler recognises W and f as destinations
f	Register file address (0x00 to 0xFF)	
k	Literal field, constant data or label 25h, txdata	

W	Working register (accumulator)	
x	Don't care location	
i	Table pointer control;	i = 0 Do not change.
		i = 1 Increment after instruction execution.

PIC16CXX

Literal and Control Operations

Hex	Mnemonic		Description	Function
3Ekk	ADDLW	k	Add literal to W	k + W » W
39kk	ANDLW	k	AND literal and W	k .AND. W » W
2kkk	CALL	k	Call subroutine	PC + 1 » TOS, k » PC
0064	CLRWDT		Clear watchdog timer	0 » WDT (and Prescaler if assigned)
2kkk	GOTO	k	Goto address (k is nine bits)	k » PC(9 bits)
38kk	IORLW	k	Incl. OR literal and W	k .OR. W » W
30kk	MOVLW	k	Move Literal to W	k » W
0009	RETFIE		Return from Interrupt	TOS »PC, 1 »GIE
34kk	RETLW	k	Return with literal in W	k » W, TOS P»C
0008	RETURN		Return from subroutine	TOS » PC
0063	SLEEP		Go into Standby Mode	0 » WDT, stop oscillator
3Ckk	SUBLW	k	Subtract W from literal	k - W » W
3Akk	XORLW	k	Exclusive OR literal and W	k .XOR. W » W

Byte Oriented Instructions

Hex	Mnemonic		Description	Function
07Ff	ADDWF	f,d	Add W and f	W + f » d
05Ff	ANDWF	f,d	AND W and f	W .AND. f » d
018F	CLRF	f	Clear f	0 » f
0100	CLRW		Clear W	0» W
09Ff	COMF	f,d	Complement f	. NOT. f » d
03Ff	DECF	f,d	Decrement f	f - 1 » d
0BFf	DECFSZ	f,d	Decrement f, skip if zero	f - 1 » d, skip if 0
0AFf	INCF	f,d	Increment f	f + 1 » d
0FFf	INCFSZ	f,d	Increment f, skip if zero	f + 1 » d, skip if 0
04Ff	IORWF	f,d	Inclusive OR W and f	W .OR. f » d
08Ff	MOVF	f,d	Move f	f » d
008F	MOVWF	f	Move W to f	W » f
0000	NOP		No operation	
0DFf	RLF	f,d	Rotate left f	
0CFf	RRF	f,d	Rotate right f	
02Ff	SUBWF	f,d	Subtract W from f	f - W » d
0EFf	SWAPF	f,d	Swap halves f	f(0:3) « f(4:7) » d
06Ff	XORWF	f,d	Exclusive OR W and f	W .XOR. f » d

Bit Oriented Operations

Hex	Mnemonic		Description	Function
10Ff	BCF	f,b	Bit clear f	0 » f(b)
14Ff	BSF	f,b	Bit set f	1 » f(b)
18Ff	BTFSC	f,b	Bit test, skip if clear	skip if f(b) = 0
1CFf	BTFSS	f,b	Bit test, skip if set	skip if f(b) = 1

PIC16C5X

Literal and Control Operations

Hex	Mnemonic		Description	Function
Ekk	ANDLW	k	AND literal and W	k .AND. W » W
9kk	CALL	k	Call subroutine	PC + 1 » TOS, k» PC
004	CLRWDT		Clear watchdog timer	0 » WDT (and Prescaler if assigned)
Akk	GOTO	k	Goto address (k is nine bits)	k » PC(9 bits)
Dkk	IORLW	k	Incl. OR literal and W	k .OR. W » W
Ckk	MOVLW	k	Move Literal to W	k » W
002	OPTION		Load OPTION Register	W » OPTION Register
8kk	RETLW	k	Return with literal in W	k » W, TOS » PC
003	SLEEP		Go into Standby Mode	0 » WDT, stop oscillator
00f	TRIS	f	Tristate port f	W » I/O control reg f
Fkk	XORLW	k	Exclusive OR literal and W	k .XOR. W » W

Byte Oriented Instructions

Hex	Mnemonic		Description	Function
1Cf	ADDWF	f,d	Add W and f	W + f » d
14f	ANDWF	f,d	AND W and f	W .AND. f » d
06f	CLRF	f	Clear f	0 » f
040	CLRW		Clear W	0 » W
24f	COMF	f,d	Complement f	.NOT. f » d
0Cf	DECF	f,d	Decrement f	f - 1 » d
2Cf	DECFSZ	f,d	Decrement f, skip if zero	f - 1 » d, skip if 0
28f	INCF	f,d	Increment f	f + 1 » d
3Cf	INCFSZ	f,d	Increment f, skip if zero	f + 1 » d, skip if 0
10f	IORWF	f,d	Inclusive OR W and f	W .OR. f » d
20f	MOVF	f,d	Move f	f » d
02f	MOVWF	f	Move W to f	W » f
000	NOP		No operation	
34f	RLF	f,d	Rotate left f	
30f	RRF	f,d	Rotate right f	
08f	SUBWF	f,d	Subtract W from f	f - W » d
38f	SWAPF	f,d	Swap halves f	f(0:3) « f(4:7) » d
18f	XORWF	f,d	Exclusive OR W and f	W .XOR. f » d

9

Bit Oriented Instructions

Hex	Mnemonic		Description	Function
4bf	BCF	f,b	Bit clear f	0 » f(b)
5bf	BSF	f,b	Bit set f	1 » f(b)
6bf	BTFSC	f,b	Bit test, skip if clear	skip if f(b) = 0
7bf	BTFSS	f,b	Bit test, skip if set	skip if f(b) = 1

PIC16C5X/PIC16CXX Special Instruction Mnemonics

These instructions are recognised by the Assembler and substituted in the program listing. They are a form of shorthand similar to Macros.

ADDCF	f,d	Add Carry to File	BTFSC	Status, Carry	
			INCF	f,d	Z
ADDCF	f,d	Add Digit Carry to File	BTFSC	Status, Digit Carry	
			INCF	f,d	Z
B	k	Branch	GOTO	k	
BC	k	Branch on Carry	BTFSC	Status, Carry	
			GOTO	k	-
BDC	k	Branch on Digit Carry	BTFSC	Status, Digit Carry	
			GOTO	k	-
BNC	k	Branch on No Carry	BTFSS	Status, Carry	
			GOTO	k	-
BNDC	k	Branch on No Digit Carry	BTFSS	Status, Digit Carry	
			GOTO	k	-
BZ	k	Branch on Zero	BTFSC	Status, Zero	
			GOTO	k	-
BNZ	k	Branch on No Zero	BTFSS	Status, Zero	
			GOTO	k	-
CLRC		Clear Carry	BCF	Status, Carry	-
CLRDC		Clear Digit Carry	BCF	Status, Digit Carry	-
CLRZ		Clear Zero	BCF	Status, Zero	-
MOVWF	f	Move File to W	MOVF	f,w	Z
NEGF	f,d	Negate File	COMF	f,f	
			INCF	f,d	Z
SETO		Set Carry	BSF	Status, Carry	
SETDC		Set Digit Carry	BSF	Status, Digit Carry	-
SETZ		Set Zero	BSF	Status, Zero	-
SKPC		Skip on Carry	BTFSS	Status, Carry	-
SKPNC		Skip on No Carry	BTFSC	Status, Carry	-
SKPDC		Skip on Digit Carry	BTFSS	Status, Digit Carry	-
SKPNDC		Skip on No Digit Carry	BTFSC	Status, Digit Carry	-
SKPZ		Skip on Zero	BTFSS	Status, Zero	-
SKPNZ		Skip on Non Zero	BTFSC	Status, Zero	-
SUBCF	f,d	Subtract Carry from File	BTFSC	Status, Carry	
			DECF	f,d	Z

SUBDCF f,d	Sub Digit Carry from File	BTFSC	Status, Digit Carry	
		DECF	f,d	Z
TSTF f	Test File	MOVF	f,f	Z

9.3 Advanced BIT Manipulation

The CCS C compiler has a number of bit manipulation functions that are commonly needed for PIC programs.

BIT_SET, BIT_CLEAR and **BIT_TEST** simply set or clear a bit in a variable or test the state of a single bit. Bits are numbered with the lowest bit (the 1 position) as 0 and the highest bit 7.

For example:

```
c='A';            // c in binary is now 01000001
BIT_SET(c,5);     // c is now 01100001 or 'a'

if(BIT_TEST(x,0))
    printf("X is odd");
else
    printf("X is even"):
```

SHIFT_LEFT and **SHIFT_RIGHT** will shift one bit position though any number of bytes. In addition it allows you to specify the bit value to put into the vacated bit position and these functions return as their value 0 or 1 representing the bit shifted out. Note that these functions consider the lowest byte in memory the LSB. The second parameter is the number of bytes and the last parameter is the new bit.

Example:

```
int x[3] = {0b10010001, 0b00011100, 0b10000001};
short bb;
        // x msb first is:  10000001 00011100 10010001
bb = shift_left(x,sizeof(x),0);
        // x msb first is:  00000010 00111001 00100010
        // bb is 1
bb = shift_left(x,sizeof(x),1);
        // x msb first is:  00000100 01110010 01000101
        // bb is 0
```

9

Note the first parameter is a pointer. In this case since x is an array the unsubscripted identifier is a pointer. If a simple variable or structure were used the & operator must be added. For example:

```
long y;
struct { int a,b,c; } z;

shift_left( &y, 2, 0);
shift_right( &z, 3, 0);
```

ROTATE_LEFT and ROTATE_RIGHT work like the shift functions above except the bit shifted out of one side gets shifted in the other side. For example:

```
int x[3] = {0b10010001, 0b00011100, 0b10000001};

        // x msb first is:  10000001 00011100 10010001
rotate_left(x,sizeof(x));
        // x msb first is:  00000010 00111001 00100011
```

The **SWAP** function swaps the upper 4 bits and lower 4 bits of a byte. For example:

```
int x;

x=0b10010110;
swap(x);
        // x is now 01101001
```

9.4 Timers

All PIC's have an 8-bit timer and some PIC's have two more advanced timers. The capabilities are as follows:

RTCC (TIMER0) 8 Bit.

May increment on the instruction clock or by an external source.

Increment may be slowed by applying a pre-scalar.

When timer overflows from 255 to 0 an interrupt can be generated (not 16C5X series).

TIMER1 **16 Bit.**

May increment on the instruction clock or by an external source.

Increment may be slowed by applying a pre-scaler.

When timer overflows from 65535 to 0 an interrupt can be generated.

In capture mode the timer1 count may be saved in another register when a pin changes. An interrupt may also be generated.

In compare mode a pin can be changed when the count reaches a preset value and an interrupt may be generated.

This timer is used as part of the PWM.

TIMER2 **8 Bit.**

May increment on the instruction clock or by an external source.

Increment may be slowed by applying a pre-scaler.

When timer overflows from 255 to 0 an interrupt can be generated.

The interrupt can be slowed by applying a post-scaler so it requires a certain number of overflows before the interrupt happens.

This timer is used as part of the PWM.

The following is a simple example using the RTCC to time how long a pulse is high:

```
#include <16C74.h>
#fuses  HS,NOWDT
#use delay(clock=1024000)
#use rs232(baud=9600,xmit=PIN_c6,rcv=PIN_c7)

main() {
    int time;

    setup_counters( RTCC_INTERNAL, RTCC_DIV_256);
            // increments 1024000/4*256 times per second
            // or every millisecond.

    while (!input(PIN_B0)) ;     // Wait for high
    set_rtcc(0);
    while (input(PIN_B0)) ;      // Wait for low
    time = get_rtcc();

    printf("High time = %u ms.",time);
}
```

The following is an example using the timer 1 capture feature to time how long it takes for pin C2 to go high after pin B0 is driven high:

```
#include <16C74.h>
#fuses  HS,NOWDT
#use delay(clock=8000000)
#use rs232(baud=9600,xmit=PIN_c6,rcv=PIN_c7)
#bit capture_1 = 0x0C.2 // PIR1 register
                // bit 2 = capture has taken place

main() {
    long time;
    setup_timer_1(T1_INTERNAL | T1_DIV_BY_2);
                // Inc's every 1 us
```

```
    setup_ccp1(CCP_CAPTURE_RE);
                // Configure CCP1 to capture rise

    capture_1=0;
    set_timer1(0);
    output_high(PIN_B0);
    while(!capture_1) ;
    time = ccp_1;

    printf("Reaction time = %lu us.",time);
}
```

9.5 A/D Conversion

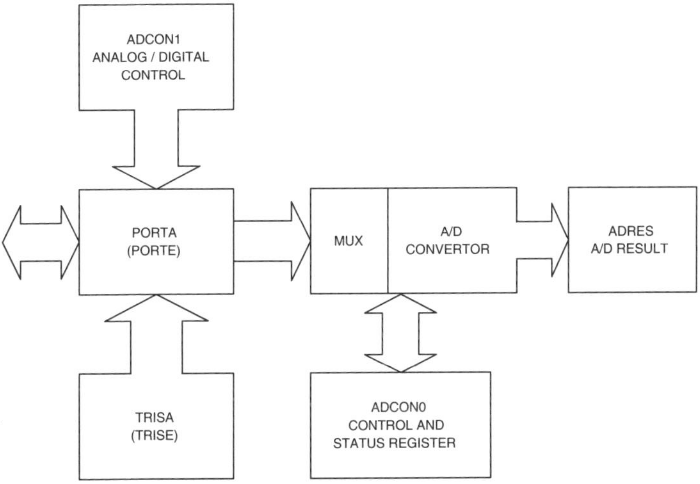

The A/D in the 16C7x and 12C67x devices has a resolution of 8 bits. This means that the voltage being measured can be resolved to one of 255 values. If a 5 volt supply is used, then the measured accuracy is 5/255 = 19.6mV over a 0 to 5 volt range. However, if the reference voltage is reduced to 2.55 volts, the resolution becomes 10mV but the working range falls to 0 to 2.55 volts.

Other Microchip parts have 10. 11, 12 and 14 bit resolution

NOTE The default for ports having both analog and digital capability is ANALOG.

It is important to note which combination of I/O lines can be used for analog and digital. The following tables are extracted from the data sheets.

[	16C72/3			]	(	16C74 ONLY	)
A0,1	**A2**	**A3**	**A5**	**E0**	**E1**	**E2**	**Vref**
A	A	A	A	A	A	A	Vdd
A	A	Vref	A	A	A	A	A3
A	D	A	A	D	D	D	Vref
D	D	Vref	A	D	D	D	A3
A	A	A	D	D	D	D	Vdd
A	A	Vref	D	D	D	D	A3
D	D	D	D	D	D	D	—-

[	16C71,710,711		]
A0,1	**A2**	**A3**	**Vref**
A	A	A	Vdd
A	A	Vref	A3
A	D	D	Vdd
D	D	D	—-

In C, the setup and operation of the A/D is simplified by ready made library routines.

set_adc_channel(0-7); select the channel for a/d conversion

setup_adc(mode); sets up the analog to digital converter. The modes are as follows:
ADC_OFF
ADC_CLOCK_DIV_2
ADC_CLOCK_DIV_8
ADC_CLOCK_DIV_32
ADC_CLOCK_INTERNAL

9

setup_adc_ports(mix); will setup the ADC pins to be analog,

digital or a combination.
The allowed combinations for mix vary depending on the chip.
The constants ALL_ANALOG and NO_ANALOGS are valid for all chips.
Some other example constants:
RA0_RA1_RA3_ANALOG
A0_RA1_ANALOG_RA3_REF

`read_adc();`

will read the digital value from the analog to digital converter.
Calls to SETUP_ADC and SET_ADC_CHANNEL should be made sometime before this function is called.
This function returns an 8 bit value 00h - FFh on parts with an 8 bit A/D converter. On parts with a greater than 8 bit A/D the value returned is always a long with the range 0000h - FFFFh.
The range may be fixed regardless of the part to aid in compatibility across parts by adding one of the following directives:

```
#Device ADC=8
#Device ADC=16
```

Example:

```
setup_adc(ALL_ANALOG);   // sets port a to all analog inputs
set_adc_channel(1);      // points a/d at channel 1

    delay_ms(5000);      // waits 5 seconds
    value = read_adc();  // reads value
    printf("A/D value = %2x\n\r", value);
                         // prints value
```

9.6 Data Comms / RS232

RS232 communications between PCs, modems etc. form part of an Engineer's life. The problem seems to arise when self built products need to be interfaced to the outside world. The permutations of 9 or 25 pins on a D connector and the software controlling communications are endless. A minimum interface can be 3 wires - Ground, Transmit and Receive - but what to do with the remaining pins? The voltage levels are between ±3 and ±15 volts allowing plenty of leeway for both drivers and receivers. When connecting equipment with RS232 interfaces, it is important to know which is classed as the Data Controlling Equipment (DCE) and which is the Data Terminal Equipment (DTE).

Cables / Connectors.

9 way D

Pin	Function	
1	Carrier Detect	in
2	Receive Data	in
3	Transmit Data	out
4	Data Terminal Ready	out
5	Ground	<>
6	Data Set Ready	in
7	Request To Send	out
8	Clear To Send	in
9	Ring Indicator	in

25 way D

Pin	Function	
1	Protective Ground	<>
2	Transmit Data	out
3	Receive Data	in
4	Request To Send	out
5	Clear To Send	in
6	Data Set Ready	in
7	Signal Ground	<>
20	Data Terminal Ready	out
22	Ring Indicator	in

The remaining pins have other functions not normally used for basic interconnection and are documented in the EIA-232-D or CCITT V24/28 specification.

Common Problems

Garbled characters	parity, speed, character length, stop bits
Lost data	flow control
Double spacing	translation of carriage returns or line feeds
Overwriting	translation of carriage returns or line feeds
No display of characters	duplex operation
Double characters	duplex operation

Data Format

Data sent via an RS232 interface follows a standard format.

Start bits	always 1 bit
Stop bits	1 or 2 bits
Data bits	7,8 bits
Parity bits	none if no error detection is required odd or even if error detection is required

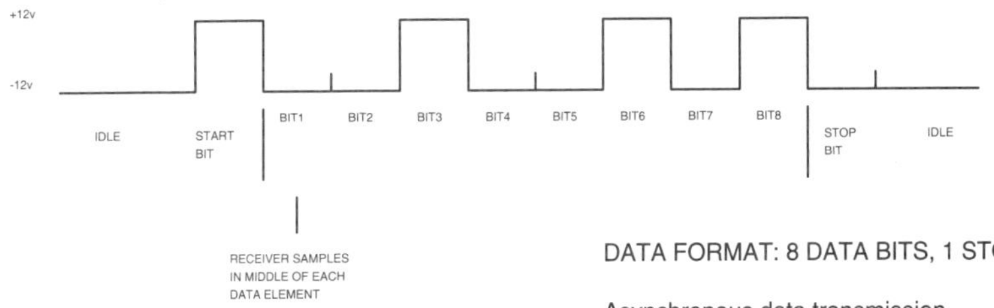

DATA FORMAT: 8 DATA BITS, 1 STOP BIT

Asynchronous data transmission

Parity

Parity checking requires the addition of an extra bit to the data byte. The parity system may be either 'odd' or 'even' and both systems give the same level of error detection.

In an odd parity system the overall count of '1's in the combined data byte plus parity bit is odd and thus with an 8 bit data byte of '10101100' the parity bit would be set to a '1'.

In an even parity system the overall count of '1's in the combined data byte plus parity bit is even and thus with an 8 bit data byte of '10101100' the parity bit would be set to a '0'.

If corruption of either data bits or of the parity bit itself takes place, when the receiver carries out the parity check the corruption will be recognised. In the event of more than one bit being corrupted it is possible that the receiver will not recognise the problem provided that the parity appears correct. So parity checking is not a cast iron method of checking for transmission errors but, in practice, in most systems it provides a reasonable level of security. The parity system does not correct errors in itself but only indicates that an error has occurred and it is up to the system software to react to the error state; in most systems this would result in a request for re transmission of the data.

The PICmicro does not have on-chip parity testing or generation, so the function needs to be generated in software. This adds an overhead to the code generated which could have a knock on effect on execution times.

Bit Rate Time Calculation

As BAUD is bits per second, each data bit has a time of $\frac{1}{\text{BAUD Rate}}$

This works out as 1200 Baud = 833µS, 2400 Baud = 416µS, 9600 Baud = 104µS

ASCII Conversion Table

Control	HEX	msb	0	1	2	3	4	5	6	7
	lsb	bits	000	001	010	011	100	101	110	111
	0	0000	NUL	DLE	SP	0	@	P	-	p
^A	1	0001	SOH	DC1	!	1	A	Q	a	q
^B	2	0010	STX	DC2	“	2	B	R	b	r
^C	3	0011	ETX	DC3	#	3	C	S	c	s
^D	4	0100	EOT	DC4	$	4	D	T	d	t
^E	5	0101	ENQ	NAK	%	5	E	U	e	u
^F	6	0110	ACK	SYN	&	6	F	V	f	v
^G	7	0111	BEL	ETB	‘	7	G	W	g	w
^H	8	1000	BS	CAN	(	8	H	X	h	x
^I	9	1001	HT	EM	)	9	I	Y	i	y
^J	A	1010	LF	SUB	*	:	J	Z	j	z
^K	B	1011	VT	ESC	+	;	K	[	k	{
^L	C	1100	FF	FS	,	<	L	\	l	
^M	D	1101	CR	GS	-	-	M	]	m	}
^N	E	1110	SO	RS	.	>	N	^	n	~
^O	F	1111	SI	US	/	?	O	_	o	DEL

The ASCII symbols in the above table are:

NUL	- Null	DLE	- Data Link Escape
SOH	- Start Of Heading	DC	- Device Control
STX	- Start Of Text	EXT	- End Of Text
EOT	- End Of Transmission	ENQ	- Enquiry
NAK	- Negative Acknowledge	ACK	- Acknowledge
SYN	- Synchronous Idle	BEL	- Bell
ETB	- End Transmission Block	BS	- Backspace
CAN	- Cancel	HT	- Horizontal Tab
EM	- End of Medium	LF	- Line Feed
SUB	- Substitute	VT	- Vertical Tab
ESC	- Escape	FF	- Form Feed
FS	- File Separator	CR	- Carriage Return
GS	- Group Separator	SO	- Shift Out
RS	- Record Separator	SI	- Shift In
US	- Unit Separator	DEL	- Delete
SP	- Space (blank)		
DC1	- Xon	DC3	- Xoff

RS232 Handshaking

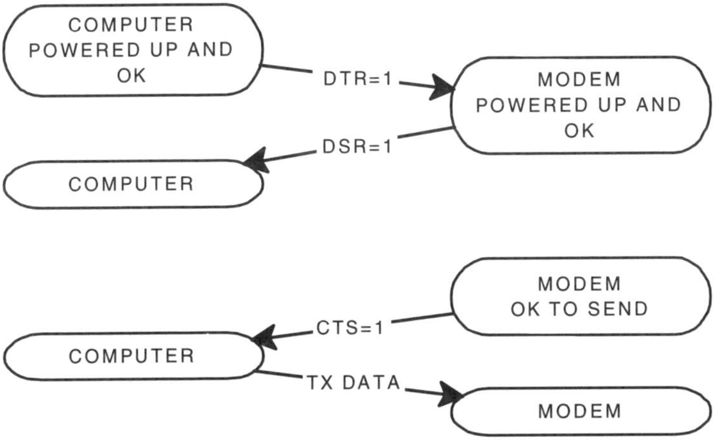

Typical Null Modem Connections

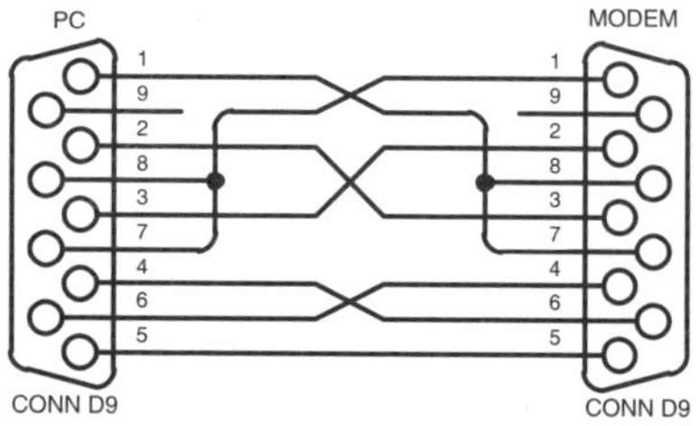

Simple RS232 Tester

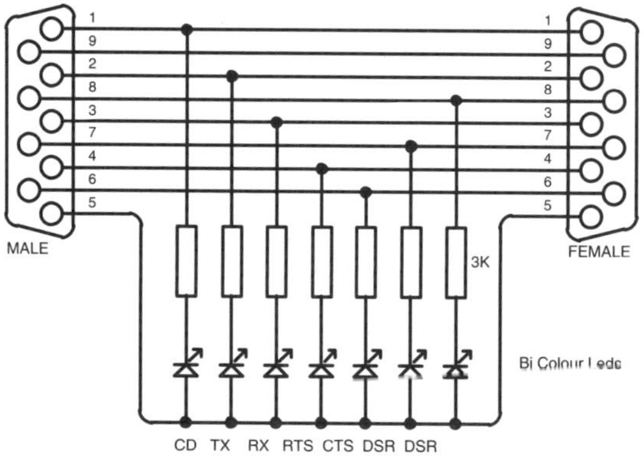

USART

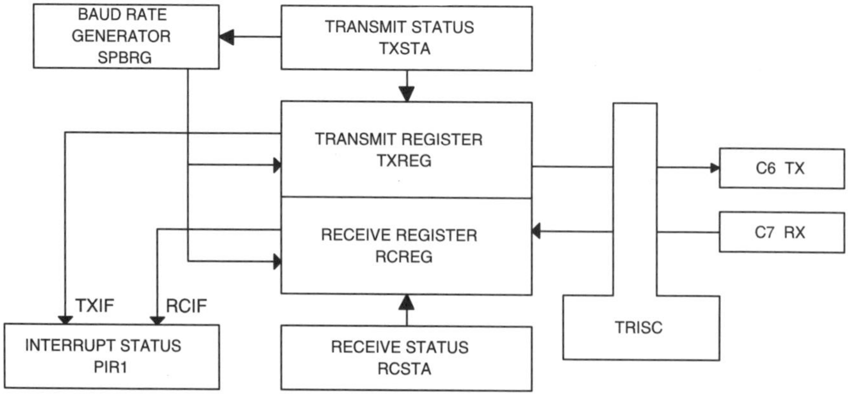

The USART operates in one of three modes - Synchronous Master,

Synchronous Slave and Asynchronous, the latter being the most common for interfacing peripherals. Besides the obvious interface to PC's and Modems, the USART can interface to A/D, D/A and EEPROM devices.

Data formats acceptable to the USART are 8 or 9 data bits, none, odd or even parity - created and tested in user software - not a hardware function and indication of over run or framing errors on the received data. In Asynchronous mode, the USART can handle full duplex communications, but only half duplex in synchronous mode.
There are pre-set functions which speed up application writing.

```
#use fixed_io(c_outputs=pin_C6) // speeds up port use
#use Delay(Clock=4000000)       // clock frequency
#use rs232(baud=4800, xmit=PIN_C6, rcv=PIN_C7)
```

The CCS compiler has the ability to use the on-board PICmicro's UART if one is present. If the UART is available in hardware, the code generated will use the existing hardware. If however the hardware is absent the resulting code generated will be larger. With the exception of the interrupt on transmit and receive, the code behaves like a hardware UART. The software UART has the ability to invert the output data levels, removing the need for an external driver/level shifter in logic level applications. This function is not available in hardware.

This code transparency enables code to be moved from on PICmicro application to another with minimal effect.

Included in the C compiler are ready made functions for communications such as:-

`getc, getch, getchar`	waits for and returns a character to be received from the RS232 rcv pin
`gets (char *string)`	reads a string of characters into the variable until a carriage return is received. A 0 terminates the string. The maximum length of characters is determined by the declared array size for the variable.

`putc putchar` — sends a single character to the RS232 xmit pin

`puts(s)` — sends a string followed by a line feed and carriage return

The function `KBHIT()` may be used to determine if a character is ready. This may be used to prevent hanging in `getc()` waiting for a character. The following is an example of a function that waits up to one half second for a character:

```
char timed_getc() {
    long timeout;

    timeout_error=FALSE;
    timeout=0;
    while(!kbhit&&(++timeout<50000))    // 1/2 second
        delay_us(10);
    if(kbhit)
        return(getc());
    else {
        timeout_error=TRUE;
        return(0);
    }
}
```

9.7 I²C Communications

I²C is a popular 2 wire communications bus to hardware devices. A single two wire I²C bus has one master and any number of slaves. The master may send or request data to/from any slave. Each slave has a unique address.

The two wires are labeled SCL and SDA. Both require a pull-up resistor (1-10K) to +5V.

Communications begins with a special start condition followed by the slave address. The LSB of this first byte indicates the direction of data transfer from this point on. Data is transferred and the receiver specifically acknowledges each byte. The receiver can slow down the transfer by holding SCL low while it is busy. After all data is transferred a stop condition is sent on the bus.

The following is an example C program that will send three bytes to the slave at address 10 and then read one byte back.

```
#include <16C74.h>
#fuses XT,NOWDT
#use delay(clock=4000000)

#use I2C(master, SCL=PIN_B0, SDA=PIN_B1)

main()
{
    int data;

    I2C_START();
    I2C_WRITE(10);
    I2C_WRITE(1);
    I2C_WRITE(2);
    I2C_WRITE(3);
    I2C_STOP();

    I2C_START();
    I2C_WRITE(11);
    data=I2C_READ();
    I2C_STOP();

}
```

9.8 SPI Communications

Like I^2C, SPI is a two or three wire communications standard to hardware devices. SPI is usually not a bus since there is one master and one slave.

One wire supplies a clock while the other sends or receives data. If a third wire is used it may be an enable or a reset. There is no standard beyond this as each device is different.

The following is C code to send a 10 bit command MSB first to a device.

Note that the shift_left function returns a single bit (the bit that gets shifted out) and this bit is the data value used in the output_bit function.

```
main()
{
   long cmd;

   cmd=0x3E1;

   for(i=1;i<=6;++i)           // Left justify cmd
      shift_left(cmd,3,0);
   output_high(PIN_B0);        // Enable device

                               // Send out 10 data bits
                               // each with a clock pulse
   for(i=1;i<=10;++i) {
      output_bit(PIN_B1, shift_left(cmd,2,0));
      output_high(PIN_B2);  // B2 is the clock
      output_low(PIN_B2);
   }

   output_low(PIN_B1);         // Disable device
   output_low(PIN_B0);
}
```

The following is C code to read a 8 bit response. Again shift_left is used and the data that is shifted in is the bit on the input pin.

```
main()
{
   int data;

   output_high(PIN_B0);        // Enable device

                               // Send a clock pulse
                               // and read a data bit
                               // eight times
   for(i=1;i<=8;++i) {
      output_high(PIN_B2);
      output_low(PIN_B2);
      shift_left(&data,1,input(PIN_B1));
   }
   output_low(PIN_B0);         // Disable device
}
```

The above are two great examples of shifting data in and out of the PIC a bit at a time. They can be easily modified to talk to a number of devices. Slower parts may need some delays to be added.

Some PIC's have built in hardware for SPI. The following is an example of using the built in hardware to write and read:

```
main()
{
   int data;

   setup_spi(SPI_MASTER | SPI_H_TO_L | SPI_CLK_DIV_16);
   output_high(PIN_B0);
   spi_write(3);
   spi_write(0xE1);
   output_low(PIN_B0);

   output_high(PIN_B0);
   data=spi_read(0);
   output_low(PIN_B0);
}
```

Note the built in hardware does have restrictions. For example the above code sent 16 bits not 10. Most SPI devices ignore all bits until the first 1 bit so this will still work.

9.9 PWM Generation

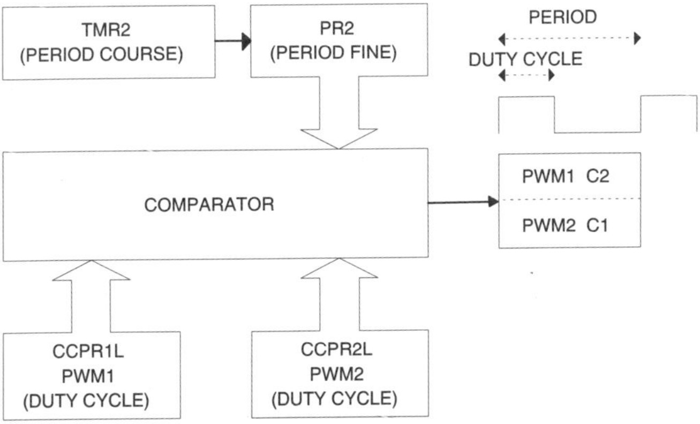

9

For PICs with PWM generation hardware, once the registers are set up, the PWM runs on its own without constant software involvement. Calculation of the PWM values is best achieved with a simple spreadsheet.

Example - PWM setup - frequency = 600Hz M/S ratio = 1:1
Prescale value = ((1/PWM Frequency) / Prescale value * (4/OSC frequency)) -1

PWM Resolution = (log(OSC freq / PWM freq)) / log 2

So for the above example, a 600Hz PWM with a 4MHz oscillator and /16 prescaller will give 103.2 to load into the PR2 register and a resolution of 12.7 bits

setup_timer_2(mode, period, postscale)
initializes timer 2 where mode is
T2_DISABLED
T2_DIV_BY_1
T2_DIV_BY_4
T2_DIV_BY_16
period is an offset value between 0 and 255 before the timer resets
postscale is a value between 0 and 16 to determine the times before an interrupt occurs

set_pwm1_duty(value) this will write the 10 bit value to the PWM

set_pwm2_duty(value) module. If only 8 bits are sent, the 2 lsb's will be ignored. Note that **value** is in the range 0 to **period**

setup_ccp1(CCP_PWM) this function will initialize the ccp in a pwm mode

setup_ccp2(CCP_PWM)

Example

```
setup_ccp1(CCP_PWM);            // sets up for pwm
setup_timer_2(T2_DIV_BY_4, 140, 0);
                                // 140 as offset, timer /4
```

```
set_pwm1_duty(70);             // 50% duty cycle ie half of
                               // 140
```

If oscillator = 4MHz, then frequency will be 1.773KHz with a potential resolution of 11 bits

The following example will generate one of two tones - determined by the value passed to the routine - for a set duration. The frequency is set with the

```
setup_timer_2(T2_DIV_BY_4, 100, 0);
```

and the duty ratio is set with

```
set_pwm1_duty(50);
```

The frequencies for the two tones are 2.475 kHz and 996 Hz. The on duration is set with a simple delay followed by setting the duty cycle to 0 - silence the output even though the PWM is still running.

```
void sound_bell(byte y)
{
    setup_ccp1(CCP_PWM);    // Configure CCP1 as a PWM
    if (y==2)
        {
  setup_timer_2(T2_DIV_BY_4, 100, 0);
        set_pwm1_duty(50);  // make this value half
                            // of tone value (100/2)
          delay_ms(200);    // 0.2 second bell from
                            // terminal
          }
    else
        {
  setup_timer_2(T2_DIV_BY_4, 250, 0);
        set_pwm1_duty(125); // make this value half
                            // of tone value (250/2)
          delay_ms(300);    // 0.3 second bell from
                            // keypad
          }
    set_pwm1_duty(0);
}
```

9

NOTE: PIC's without PWM hardware cannot have the function generated by software unlike the USART function. However, PWM like functions can be simulated.

For example:

```
while(true){
    output_high(PIN_B0);
    delay_us(500);
    output_low(PIN_B0);
    delay_us(500);
}
```

Will generate a 1 kHz square ware. However, the PIC is dedicated to this operation and can not do anything else. This can be overcome by toggling the pin in an interrupt routine set to go off at a fixed rate.

9.10 LCD Display driving

One of the most common display interfaces to PIC based designs is an LCD display based on the Hitachi controller. There are two modes of operation, 4 and 8 wire, with the option of write/delay or write/check busy when sending data to the display. It is an advantage to have a copy of the current display data sheet when writing software showing correct timing and setup codes.

A typical interface circuit is shown below. The PIC interfaces to the display in a 4 bit mode. Register Select (RS) changes between control and data register banks within the display and the Enable (E) is used to strobe data into the display. In the 4 bit mode, the most significant nibble is sent first.

The Initalisation code looks like:

```
byte CONST LCD_INIT_STRING[5] = {0x28, 0x06, 0x0c,
0x01, 0x80};
                        // Send to the LCD
                        // to start it up - see data sheet
void lcd_init(byte x)
```

```
{
    byte i;
    set_tris_b(0);     // make port all output
    cont.rs = 0;
    cont.en = 0;
    delay_ms(15);      // delay
    for(i=1;i<=3;++i)
  {
        lcd_send_nibble(3);
        delay_ms(5);
      }
    lcd_send_nibble(2);
      for(i=0;i<=4;i++)
           lcd_send_byte(0,LCD_INIT_STRING[i]);
}
```

Sending a byte of information to the display on nibble at a time looks like:

```
void lcd_send_byte(byte address, byte n)
{
  cont.rs = address;
  delay_cycles(1);
  delay_cycles(1);
  cont.en = 0;
  lcd_send_nibble(n >> 4);      // shift upper nibble
                                // 4 places
  lcd_send_nibble(n & 0xf);     // mask off upper
                                // nibble
       delay_ms(10);
}
```

The function `lcd_send_nibble` does the strobe function:

```
void lcd_send_nibble(byte n)
{
   lcd_data = n;           // place data on port
   delay_cycles(1);        // delay 1 cycle
   cont.en = 1;            // set enable high
   delay_us(2);            // delay 2uS
   cont.en = 0;            // set enable low
}
```

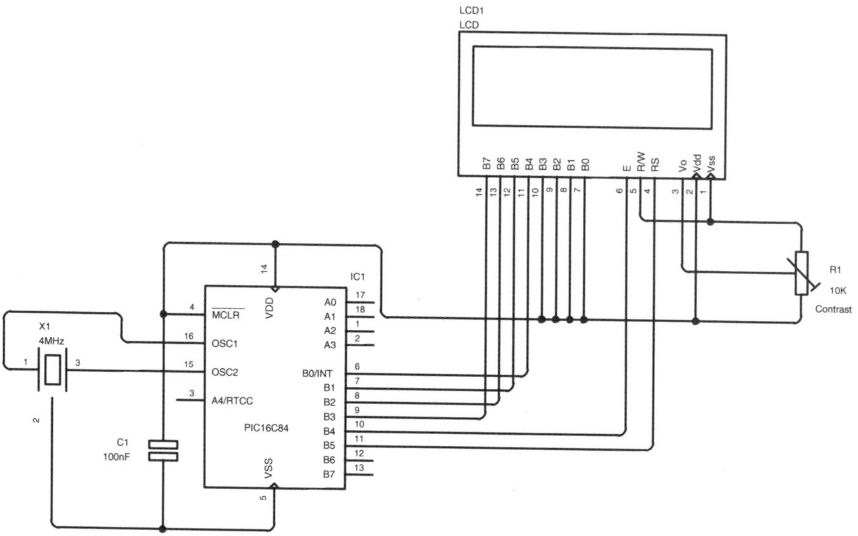

Another function which is useful when dealing with LCD displays is the scroll. This is not the inbuilt left/right scroll, but a software scroll up function. The following example is used to place the latest text on the bottom line of a 4 line display and scroll the previous line and the other 3 up one. The top line then scrolls off the display and is lost.

```
byte Line1[0x10];          // setup arrays to hold data
byte Line2[0x10];
byte Line3[0x10];
byte Line4[0x10];
memcpy(Line1, Line2, 0x10); // transfer data from one array
memcpy(Line2, Line3, 0x10); // to the next
memcpy(Line3, Line4, 0x10); // and again
memset(Line4, 0x20,  0x10); // and clear bottom line
lcd_same_line(0);           // go to start of display
for (i=0;i<=0x0f;++i)
     {
     k= Line1[i];           // send data from line1
     lcd_send_byte(1,k);    // memory array to display
     }
// repeat for other 3 lines
```

9.11 Interrupts

Interrupts can come from a wide range of sources within the PIC and also from external events. When an interrupt occurs, the PIC hardware follows a fixed pattern as shown below.

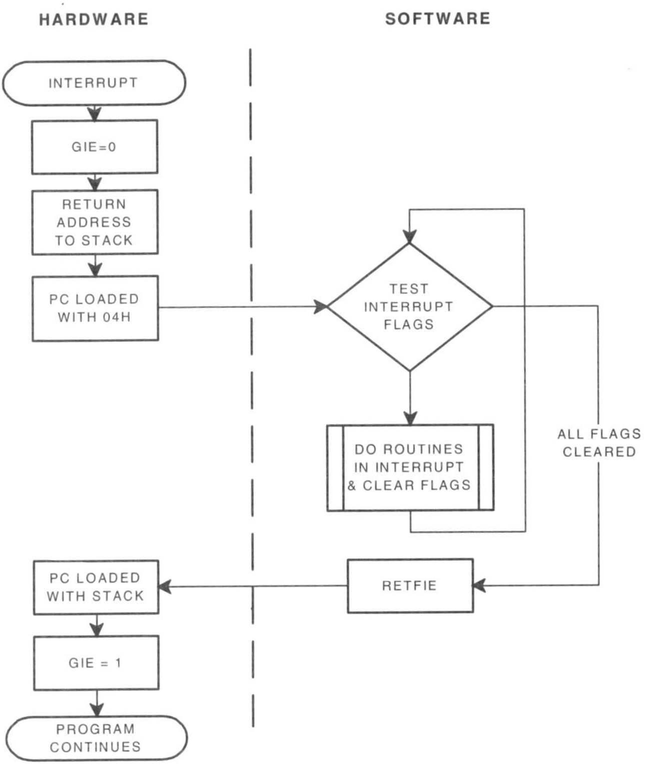

The hardware side is completely under PIC control, the software is all your responsibility. When an interrupt occurs, the first step is to test to determine if the source is the desired one or, in the case of multiple interrupts, which one to handle first etc.

Depending on which PIC is used in a design, the type and number of interrupts will vary. The PIC16C5x series have no interrupts and software written for these products will have to perform a software poll. Some of the interrupt sources are shown below, but refer to the data sheet for the latest information.

`#priority` sets up the order of the interrupt priority eg

```
#priority rtcc, rb, tmr0, portb
```

`#int_global` - use with care to create your own interrupt handler. The main save and restore of registers and startup code is not generated.

`#int_default` is used to capture unsolicited interrupts from sources not setup for interrupt action. Examine the interrupt flags to determine which false interrupt has been triggered.

`#int_xxx` - where xxx is the desired interrupt eg

```
#int_rda                    // enable usart receive
                            // interrupt
rs232_handler()             // interrupt driven data read
                            // and store
{
b=getch();                  // load character
Buffer[Buff+1] = b;         // store character in memory
Buff++;                     // increment pointer
}
```

```
enable_interrupts (level);
disable_interrupts (level);
```

these functions set or clear the respective interrupt enable flags so interrupts can be turned on and off during the program execution.

```
ext_int_edge (edge);
```

This is used to select the incoming polarity on Port B bit 0 when used as an external interrupt. The edge can be `l_to_h or h_to_l` .

This example forces an interrupt on receipt of a character received via the USART. The character is placed in a buffer and the buffer incremented ready for the next character. This function is extracted from an LCD display program as the characters are received faster than the display can handle them.

```
#int_rda
  rs232_handler()        // interrupt driven data
                         // read and store
  {
  b=getch();             // load character
  Buffer[Buff+1] = b;    // store character in memory
        Buff++;          // increment pointer
  }
main()
{
     enable_interrupts(INT_RDA);
     enable_interrupts(GLOBAL);
   do {
while (True);
}
```

Include Libraries

These libraries add the icing on the cake for a C programmer. They contain all the string handling and math's functions that will be used in a program. The various libraries are included as and when the user requires them.

CTYPE.H contains several traditional macros as follows:

Returns a TRUE if:

isalnum(x)	x is an alphanumetic value ie 0..9, 'A'..'Z', or 'a'..'z'
isalpha(x)	x is an alpha value ie 'A'..'Z' or 'a'..'z'
isdigit(x)	x is a numeric value ie '0'..'9'
islower(x)	x is a lower case value ie 'a'..'z'
isupper(x)	x is an upper case value ie 'A'..'Z
isspace(x)	x is a space
isxdigit(x)	x is a hexadecimal digit ie '0'..'9', 'A'..'F', or 'a'..'f'

STDLIB.H contains

f = abs(x)	returns the absolute value of x
i = atoi(char *ptr)	returns the ASCII representation of the character as int

i = atol(char *ptr)	returns the ASCII representation of the character as long
i = labs (i)	returns the absolute value of a long integer x

MATH.H

Holds all the complicated math's functions. Examination of this file gives an insight into how the mathematical functions operate. In all cases the value returned is a floating point number.

l = sqrt(x)	returns the non-negative square root of the float value x
l = sin(x)	returns the sine value of float x
l = asin(x)	returns the arc sine value of float x
l = tan(x)	returns the tan value of float x
l = atan(x)	returns the sine value of float x
l = cos(x)	returns the cos value of float x
l = acos(x)	returns the arc cos value of float x
l = floor(x)	returns the largest value not greater than the value of float x
l = ceil(x)	returns the smallest value greater than the value of float x
l = exp(x)	returns the exponential value of float x
l = log(x)	returns the log to base e value of float x
l = log10(x)	returns the log to base 10 value of float x

Where Next

What do I need to start development ?

The minimum items required to start PIC development work are :-
An IBM compatible PC - running Windows 3.1, 95 or 98
C Compiler

If you then wish to take the development from paper to a hardware design, you will need :-
A programmer - for reliability and support get the PICSTART Plus which covers all the Microchip devices and is upgradable.
A development board or hardware starter kit - to save time trying to debug software and hardware.
Some EPROM (windowed) versions of the PIC to be used - say 3/5 to save time when they are being erased.
An EPROM eraser - build or buy.
If developing with the 16C84 (EEPROM), you don't need an eraser as the device is electrically erasable - i.e. no window.

Development Path

Zero Cost Demo versions of the C compiler
Starter PICSTART Plus Programmer + C Compiler + PIC sample.
Intermediate Microchip ICD for 16C87X family.
Serious In Circuit Emulator (ICE) - ICE PIC or PIC MASTER - allows debugging of hardware and software at same time. You need a programmer to go with the ICE - see catalogue for part numbers.

Support Products from Bluebird Electronics

The latest range of products can be found on our web site.

PIC Millennium Board contains all the necessary components to start learning the intricacies of the PIC and is aimed at both Engineers and Students. Students can use the board to help form the core of their learning experience and also use it in "real world" applications as they move into industry. The board is laid out in an uncluttered way with none of the peripheral devices or I/O pins being dedicated. This concept enables maximum flexibility for project development.

PIC in a Box - A complete starter kit for those intending to work with the PIC. PIC in a Box comprises PICSTART Plus, Beginners Guide to the PIC, PIC Cookbook Vol 1, Project Board, PIC Soft with additional projects aimed at the absolute beginner, starter guidance notes. 16Cxx **(8/18 pin) Hardware Starter Kit** - PCB, 8 leds, regulator, 4MHz crystal, reset components.

16C55/57 Hardware Starter Kit - PCB, 8 leds, regulator, 4MHz crystal, reset components.

Project Board 2 (18 pin PIC's) - PCB, leds, regulator, push buttons, speaker, thermistor, dip switch, PP3 battery holder, 4MHz crystal, reset switch - ideal starter kit for students or engineers.

40 pin 16CXX Hardware Starter Kit - PCB, leds, regulator, push buttons, RS232 interface, EEPROM socket, 200 hole patch area, PIC Soft disk.

PIC Converter - A pin conversion adapter to allow 16C63/73 devices (28 pin) to be used with the above 16C64/74 Hardware Starter Kit.

PLCC Programmer Adapter - Enables 44 pin PIC's (not 17Cxx) to be programmed on the PIC START Plus .

PLCC Interface Cable - Enables either the ICE PIC or PIC MASTER to interface with 44 pin PLCC sockets on target board.

Pointers to get started

Start off with a simple program - don't try to debug 2000 lines of code in one go.

Use known working hardware - Bluebird starter kits for example - for the initial design phase to save debug time.

Have a few windowed PICs to hand when developing to save time waiting for erasure

If using the PIC Start Plus (programmer only) you will need to use the program - test - modify process - so allow extra development time.

An ICE will speed up development and save the company money - if an engineer costs his company $400 per day, three days wasted trying to sort out a bug without an ICE and the ICE would have paid for itself, and met a deadline!

Use some form of I/O map when starting your design to speed up port identification and function

Draw a software functional block diagram to enable modular code writing

Comment the software as it's written. It is meaningless the following day or if read by another
Write, test and debug each module stage by stage
Update documentation at the end of the process
Attend a Microchip approved Training Workshop

What happens when my program won't run ?

Check the following:-
Has the oscillator configuration been set correctly when you programmed the PIC?
Was the watchdog enabled when not catered for in the software?
Have all the ports been initialised correctly?
On 16C7x devices, check if the ADCON1 register is configured as analog or digital.
Ensure the data registers are set to a known condition.
Make sure no duplication of names given to variables, registers and labels.
Is the reset vector correct, especially if code has been moved from one PIC family to another?

Reference Literature

Microchip Data sheets and CD ROM for latest product information.
CCS Reference Manual.
Microchip MPLAB Documentation and Tutorial

Some good reference books on C in general

Turbo C - Kelly & Pohl	0-8053-7880-4
An Introduction to Programming in C - Kelly & Pohl	0-8053-6860-4
C Programming Guide - Purdum	0-88022-157-7
The C Programming Language - Kernighan & Ritchie	0-13-110163-3

Hex Conversion Table

	0	**1**	**2**	**3**	**4**	**5**	**6**	**7**	**8**	**9**	**A**	**B**	**C**	**D**	**E**	**F**
0	0	1	2	3	4	5	6	7	8	9	10	11	12	13	14	15
1	16	17	18	19	20	21	22	23	24	25	26	27	28	29	30	31
2	32	33	34	35	36	37	38	39	40	41	42	43	44	45	46	47
3	48	49	50	51	52	53	54	55	56	57	58	59	60	61	62	63
4	64	65	66	67	68	69	70	71	72	73	74	75	76	77	78	79
5	80	81	82	83	84	85	86	87	88	89	90	91	92	93	94	95
6	96	97	98	99	100	101	102	103	104	105	106	107	108	109	110	111
7	112	113	114	115	116	117	118	119	120	121	122	123	124	125	126	127
8	128	129	130	131	132	133	134	135	136	137	138	139	140	141	142	143
9	144	145	146	147	148	149	150	151	152	153	154	155	156	157	158	159
A	160	161	162	163	164	165	166	167	168	169	170	171	172	173	174	175
B	176	177	17S	179	180	181	182	183	184	185	186	187	188	189	190	191
C	192	193	194	195	196	197	198	199	200	201	202	203	204	205	206	207
D	208	209	210	211	212	213	214	215	216	217	218	219	220	221	222	223
E	224	225	226	227	228	229	230	231	232	233	234	235	236	237	238	239
F	240	241	242	243	244	245	246	247	248	249	250	251	252	253	254	255

HEX		**Binary**			**Decimal**
	8	4	2	1	
0	0	0	0	0	0
1	0	0	0	1	1
2	0	0	1	0	2
3	0	0	1	1	3
4	0	1	0	0	4
5	0	1	0	1	5
6	0	1	1	0	6
7	0	1	1	1	7
8	1	0	0	0	8
9	1	0	0	1	9
A	1	0	1	0	10
B	1	0	1	1	11
C	1	1	0	0	12
D	1	1	0	1	13
E	1	1	1	0	14
F	1	1	1	1	15

Contact Information

CCS	Web:	www.ccsinfo.com (compiler & support)
	Email:	ccs@ccsinfo.com

See the CCS customer exchange area as an excellent source of help.

Microchip	Web:	www.microchip.com (for MPLAB & product information)
RF Solutions	Web:	www.rfsolutions.co.uk (In Circuit Emulators and RF products)

Authors Information

Nigel Gardner is an Electronic Engineer of over 20 years industrial experience in various fields. He owns Bluebird Electronics specialising in LCD display products, custom design work, PIC Support Products and Microchip Training Workshops.

Nigel is a member of the Microchip Consultants Group.

Tel: 01380 827080
Fax: 01380 827082
Email: info@bluebird-electronics.co.uk
WEB: www.bluebird-electronics.co.uk

NOTES